HUNGRY SOULS

Hungry Souls

Supernatural Visits, Messages, and Warnings from Purgatory

Gerard J. M. van den Aardweg

Janusz Rosikoń, Poland
PHOTOGRAPHS

TAN Books
An Imprint of Saint Benedict Press, LLC
Charlotte, North Carolina
2012

CONTENTS

ACKNOWLEDGMENTS

We want to express our special gratitude to the vicar of the church of the Sacred Heart of Suffrage in Rome, Father Domenico Santangini, M.S.C; to the curator of the monastery of the Paulinian Fathers in Czestochowa, Father Melchior Królik; and to Franco Palmieri and Wlodzimierz Redzioch in Rome, for their kind help and services.

We are still alive and we are hungry for love!

—Message from a Holy Soul

Vanity it is: to be only mindful of the present life, and not fix one's eyes on the future.

—Thomas à Kempis, *Imitatio Christi*

INTRODUCTION

PURGATORY AND THE PARANORMAL

"*F*or those who [at death] find themselves in a condition of being open to God, but still imperfectly, the journey towards full beatitude requires a purification, which the faith of the Church illustrates in the doctrine of purgatory."

This is how Pope John Paul II explains why Purgatory is necessary, for, he continues, we are called "to be perfect like the heavenly Father during our earthly life . . . sound and flawless before God the Father 'at the coming of our Lord Jesus with all his saints' (1 Thess 3:12)."[1]

Here John Paul reaffirms the old wisdom concerning the existence of a "state of purification" after death. Purification means atonement for sins and their effects on the soul. It is not a painless, automatic process of "growing" the soul, of attaining full "self-realization" through the acquisition of ever more insight after death, as is the soothing theory of some spiritualists. It is not an accumulation of learning, through a series of "reincarnations," until some point of perfect wisdom is reached, as in the fantasy of some Western New

---

* References throughout this book can be found in the Bibliography.

Age disciples. Such are childish attempts to suppress man's deep awareness that the basic dimension determining his destiny in the next world is not knowledge or experience but moral purity: sin, and the traces it leaves on the soul, versus holiness.

In our culture today, of the three destinations that traditional Christian doctrine teaches may follow death and judgment—Heaven, Hell, and Purgatory—only belief in Heaven or some such happy state has widely survived. The prevailing cheap optimism holds that (if there is anything at all across the threshold of death) the life of practically everybody automatically ends up in a state of bliss. De-christened and inwardly impoverished Western man may acknowledge having his imperfections and shortcomings but doesn't look upon himself as sinful. To him, atonement for or purification from sin is a "medieval" idea.

Already 150 years ago, Cardinal John Henry Newman saw the rise of this superficial, humanist mentality:

> We are cherishing a shallow religion, a hollow religion, which will not profit us in the day of trouble. The age [our age considerably more than his!] loves an exclusively cheerful religion. It is determined to make religion bright and sunny and joyous, whatever the form of it which it adopts. And it will handle the Catholic doctrine in the same spirit . . . we take what is beautiful and attractive, shrink from what is stern and painful.[2]

Purgatory (to say nothing of Hell), penance, expiation, God's holy Justice: these just do not fit in with today's cheerfully cheap religiosity. However, the truth remains that man has to be "sound and flawless before God the Father" when, after death, he appears before Him to render an account of his life. Only holy souls have direct access to the blissful abode where "nothing unclean shall enter."[3] Therefore, "every trace of attachment to evil must be eliminated, every imperfection of the soul corrected."[4] The place for this correction of the soul's imperfections is Purgatory.

This is not only a profound and holy mystery but also an appalling mystery, whose frightening aspects cannot be glossed over. But the reality should not terrify us. John Paul II continues, "One last important aspect which the Church's tradition has always pointed out *should*

Facade of the church of the Sacred Heart of Suffrage in Rome.

(on the previous page)
Church of the Sacred Heart of Suffrage, facade: Statues of saints who, in one way or another, are important with respect to purgatory. From left to right: St. Augustine, St. Peter, St. Joseph (great intercessor for the suffering souls); in the middle: the Blessed Virgin, the principal helper of the souls; St. John, St. Paul (texts of both saints refer to Purgatory), St. Odilon of Cluny (998–1048; this abbot took initiative for the institution of All Souls Day on November 2).

be re-proposed today: the dimension of 'communio' . . . the ecclesiastical solidarity which works through prayer, prayers of suffrage, and love."[5] Here John Paul teaches us that penance and pain in Purgatory are mitigated by the comfort of mercy. In the final analysis, Purgatory is the mercy of Christ working through his Mystical Body, the Church.

Bas-relief above the central entrance of the church: The suffering souls in Purgatory. Surrounding text: "Requiem aeternam dona eis, Domine. Et lux perpetua luceat eis." ("Lord, give them eternal rest, and may the perpetual light shine upon them," from the Requiem Mass.) Horizontal text: "Cordi Jesu SS pro animabus igne purgatorio expiandis" ("To the Most Sacred Heart of Jesus, for the souls that must expiate in the fire of purgatory").

✻ ✻ ✻

Close to the Vatican, alongside the Tiber in Rome, stands a beautiful neo-Gothic Church (the only one in that style in the whole
city), which is devoted to the Sacred Heart of Suffrage—suffrage
in the meaning of help to the souls in Purgatory. In a room in the
sacristy are exhibited a small number of strange, fascinating "relics": objects bearing visible, physical traces left by souls in Purgatory. The collection is known as the *Piccolo Museo del Purgatorio*
(Little Museum of Purgatory). The *Museo* and the church of the
Sacred Heart of Suffrage represent two sides of Purgatory: the collection offers impressive bits of tangible evidence for the harrowing
existence of the souls there, while the church itself displays the
Christian comfort of the mercy and charity for the suffering souls
as practiced since time immemorial by the Catholic Church. The
great central triptych in the church, representing the Sacred Heart,
the poor (or holy) souls, and various saints, has even been called
"a visual compendium of Catholic doctrine on purgatory" by Pope
Benedict XV.[6]

The church is a monument in honor of the mercy of the divine-
human Heart of Christ for the souls in Purgatory and, at the same
time, an invitation to the faithful to practice charity for them in
union with His merciful heart, for the devotion to the suffering
souls is inextricably linked to the devotion of the Sacred Heart.
That has been made especially clear by St. Margaret Mary Alacoque, the apostle of the devotion to the Sacred Heart. As Father
John Croiset wrote,

> The revelations she received about the sufferings of these souls,
> about our Divine Lord's tender love for them and His eager desire
> for their deliverance, of the great efficacy of the devotion to the
> Sacred Heart for their early release, and the fact that . . . (she)
> combined these two devotions so intimately in her own person,
> indicate that there is such a close connection between the two
> devotions that the devotion to the souls in Purgatory may be said
> to form a part of the devotion to the Sacred Heart.[7]

The Sacred Heart, the Blessed Virgin, St. Joseph, the angels, saints, holy Mass, and the souls in purgatory. Painting by Giuseppe and Alessandro Catani above the main altar in the church of the Sacred Heart of Suffrage. Pope Benedict XV called this painting "a visual compendium of Catholic doctrine on purgatory."

Stained-glass window in the church of the Sacred Heart of Suffrage representing St. Thomas Aquinas (left) and St. Bonaventura (right), theologians of purgatory and advocates of the devotion to the poor souls.

Christ appears to St. Margaret-Mary Alacoque. Painting above the altar of the saint in the same church.

Church of the Sacred Heart of Suffrage. "Mortem nostrum moriendo destruxit": by offering up the merits of the Passion and death of Christ to God, the faithful can alleviate or shorten the suffering of the souls in purgatory.

* * *

The "paranormal" evidence displayed in the Little Museum of the church and some additional evidence, notably the burned-in hand in the *corporale* of Czestochowa in Poland, are instrumental in developing devotion to the suffering souls. It brings us nearer to the reality of Purgatory by allowing us a closer look into this awful abyss of purification.

These evidences also appeal to the modern mind, with its preference for concrete proof and witness testimony. They bear the signature of souls who have appeared from Purgatory to ask for mercy, revealing something about themselves and their condition of suffering and doing penance.

The paranormal specimens in the *Museo del Purgatorio* and an item like the "hand of Czestochowa" are the best-documented paranormal evidence to be found in relation to contacts with the dead. The authenticity of the apparition stories linked to each of the specimens in the museum has been verified by critical priests, theologians, and trustworthy witnesses. And despite their relative rarity, they are not the only ones in existence. Uncritical credulity is of course not the right mind-set to approach them, but it is no less narrow-minded to exclude beforehand the occurrence of events other than those of everyday experience, presumptively concluding that they must be the products of superstition or even fraud. G.K. Chesterton rightly noted (in *The Incredulity of Father Brown*), "It is natural to believe in the supernatural. It never feels natural to accept only natural things."

Our present tour of Purgatory, then, will be mainly a tour of human experiences, of trustworthy apparitions of souls from the afterlife. Although we shall occasionally refer to theology, theology is not our prime focus here. But then, it is clear that many of these apparitions from the dead are nonetheless full of theological wisdom, for all reliable reports of apparitions from the dead are interesting, but the fact is that the overwhelming majority of the more elaborate, instructive, and well-documented apparitions come from the Catholic world. There seems to be a message in that fact.

The program of this book is as follows: after a few introductory considerations on the notion of Purgatory in history and on apparitions of the dead in general, we'll enter the *Museo del Purgatorio* in Rome to examine the individual items of its collection, presented to the reader by the artful work of photographer Janusz Rosikoń that will lead us to the inspection of more such pieces of evidence, beginning with the relic of Czestochowa and then to some singularly informative cases of apparitions of souls from Purgatory in the 20th century. As we try to penetrate a little into this too-often forgotten part of the next world, we may become more keenly aware that the souls in Purgatory are in need of our help and are too often forsaken.

✳   ✳   ✳

Confronted with some of the pieces of evidence from the *Museo* and with the stories behind them, many people understandably react with a shiver. Manifestations from beyond the tomb are indeed frightening, in particular visible apparitions, ghosts, or phantoms. And these manifestations are not only frightening when they are of demonic origin; even apparitions from heaven may incite fear. Moreover, the signals from Purgatory point to grievous suffering.

But when looking at the pictures of burned-in hands or when meditating on the stories of apparitions from Purgatory, we must keep in mind that these souls seldom unfold their whole inner condition, if such a thing were possible at all. They show only the face of their profound misery, presumably because the main reasons for appearing are to ask for mercy and to awaken the awareness of the seriousness of sin in the living, urging them to strive after holiness. But it is more difficult to understand—for the next world really transcends our earthly perceptions and experiences—that Purgatory has simultaneously a totally different dimension: the "poor souls" or "holy souls" seem to experience unimaginable consolations and joys as well. Tangible manifestations and communications from Purgatory are, so to speak, coded in the language of images and words we can understand, but that is only an approximation of the language of the hereafter. We know that grief and joy can coexist in the soul on earth, but how the extremes of suffering and rejoicing can go together in Purgatory is beyond normal human experience. Yet on balance, the place or state of purification, of God's fathomless justice, is at the same time a place or state of God's mercy, of hope, inner peace, and joy.

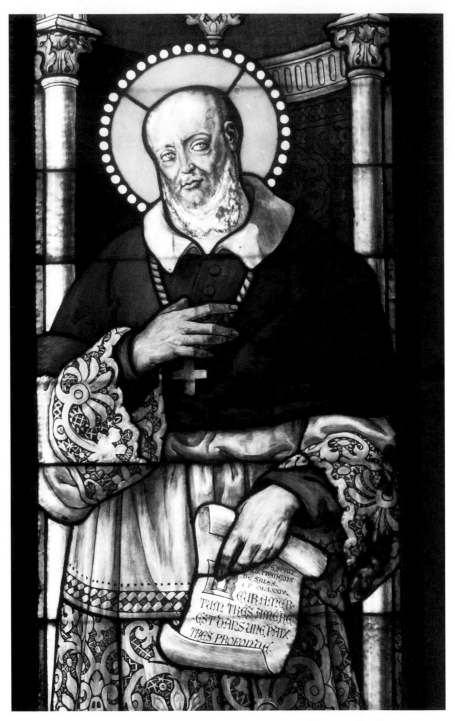

St. Francis de Sales. Window in the church of the Sacred Heart of Suffrage.

In the same church: Queen of the Rosary, help of the suffering souls.

St. Francis of Sales, a Doctor of the Church who can be called an authority on this issue, was amazingly outspoken: "The thought of Purgatory is productive rather of consolation than of terror," he wrote. "Great as the torments of purgatory are . . . the interior consolations granted there are nevertheless so ineffable that no earthly bliss and enjoyment can equal them."[8]

CHAPTER 1

THE NEAR-DEATH
EXPERIENCE—AND BEYOND

*N*ear-death experiences are well established. A percentage (5, 10, or even 20 percent, depending on the group under study) of people who have come back from the threshold of death—from a state characterized by a standstill of heartbeat and respiration, deep coma, falling away of important reflexes, and disturbed or diminished brain functioning—report impressive experiences as if they had been in a waking state. Many "saw" their body and the things that happened around it as if from above and could hear what was said around it. Then they went through a dark tunnel into a bright light, experienced an overview of their whole life, and/or met with an "entity of light" or with deceased relatives.[1]

This is all very suggestive of their having set a few initial steps into the afterlife, of having had a glimpse of what comes after death. In many instances, the people who returned from the near-death situation appear to have been deeply influenced for the better. They come back to life less self-centered, more intent on loving other people, and more positive toward religion.

One of the best elaborated and informative cases that can be found in the literature is the autobiography of the German-Austrian industrial manager Hellmut Laun, who had such an experience during an operation after an automobile accident in 1929. When the archbishop of Vienna, Cardinal Franz König, asked him to write an account of the experience and his subsequent investigations of it, by which his life had been completely changed, his first reaction was negative: "on the one hand, because it is always hard to convey things that concern one's own soul to a greater public; on the other, because it is difficult to make comprehensible the kind of experiences such as fell to my share." This is a typical reaction. People with supernatural experiences want to protect their inner privacy. Many years later, he nevertheless decided to make his story public, hoping his testimony might help others "who seek God with a sincere of heart," for his near-death experience had opened up for himself the way to God and the Church.[2]

The following fragments of his account are of special interest. While under an anesthetic during the emergency operation, Hellmut Laun's life became endangered. The anesthetist told him he was concerned that Laun "would not come back" from the procedure. As for Laun himself,

> Time and space ceased to exist, the contact with the environment was broken off, every feeling extinguished. But now I experienced something extraordinary: at first faintly, yet increasingly more clearly it dawned upon me that I "was there" again. I woke up as it were in an immaterial space separated from the world and captured myself as "I." My self-awareness was absolutely identical with my being a person in the world and yet of a different nature. It is difficult to find the fitting words for that. I would rather say: I perceived again like previously in the world, but receptive, not of myself, by my own will, and yet actively, intensively, and with awe.

Note that his personal identity, his ego, his soul, was just the same, fully intact. He continued,

In this immaterial space (space not in the earthly sense) I discerned in the far distance, unclear in the beginning, a spiritual center, like a light of tremendous intensity, a Center unto which everything in that space was ordered. My "spiritual eye," the center of my person, directed itself, as fascinated, to that still far-away center, and merely seeing it aroused in me a deep yearning to come nearer to it, as to the ultimate, most blissful goal. It looked as if everything I had ever longed and wished for in my life was put together there as in a focus, and alive in a fullness that exceeded all imagination, and orientated to that Center; and as if each creature couldn't but strive after the most intimate bond with just that ravishing spiritual Center. Its perception was immediately accompanied with a profound feeling of happiness; for I noticed that I moved towards that most intensely desired Center, that I got nearer to it. Not in a straight line, but . . . in circles that became narrower at each revolution. That way I came nearer and nearer to the Center. At each revolution It became more distinct to me, more ravishing, and at the same time the yearning to attain this desired Goal deepened, became ever more intense. It was as if I increasingly comprehended with full clarity that no earthly good had ever sent me that much into raptures, and could have sent me into raptures, as this incomprehensible Light.

Today, after so many years, I would say that from this mysterious Center emanated an infinite fullness of life, a mysterious Everything-in-All. In that yearning to wholly arrive at this Center, there was no trace of annihilation, no thought of being extinguished in this tremendous Sun, out of which boundless power seemed to irradiate. Very clearly joined with these raptures at coming nearer was the certainty that my own "I" would find its fulfillment there.

Laun wrote this many years after the fact, from memory. The fascinating thing is that his memory, apparently an immaterial faculty, retains this experience, this perception of nonmaterial realities, at all. He translates his retained perception of immaterial realities back into earthly words and material images: distance, space, Center, Sun. The words and images he uses do not transmit these realities directly; they can only approximate them. However, irrespective of these limitations, it is clear that the basic dimensions of the psyche turn out to be the same in the hereafter as in this life: the I, consciousness, thinking, feeling, longing for happiness and fulfillment; in other words, by death "life is changed, not taken away." *Vita mutatur, non tollitur.*

Laun also gets a glimpse of a departed soul who was detained on the spot where it found itself and could not come nearer to the Center:

> On my way to the Center I saw—as I clearly remember— a man; not in his body, and yet I saw him very real. This man, or rather this spiritual being, had its gaze fixed on that Center with an unquenchable craving, with a longing that at the same time caused deep pains because something, whatever it might be, impeded him to come nearer to the rapturous goal, if only a hair's breadth. He was pin-pointed as it were and couldn't move any more, although he pined for it, as I could read from his expression, with all passion, with his whole soul. . . . When I look back today, only this face, stiffened in pain, is clearly in my memory.

He thinks the unhappy figure was Voltaire. The suggestion is that he was in Hell, as there was no hope for him ever to come nearer to the Center.[3] Anyhow, Laun "saw" the suffering of that happiness-thirsty soul who can see the water but cannot get at it. In Laun's vision, there was no fire, no flames. But that need not mean that the soul in Hell—or in Purgatory, for that matter—is not ablaze with a real and/or mystical fire. In a certain sense, extreme longing and a feeling of burning converge. The extreme yearning of souls in Hell or Purgatory may feel more like a scorching fire than an earthly fire to our body. As we shall see, this is the view of St. Catherine of Genoa, the "theologian of Purgatory."

> With each further revolution, with increasing approximation, the longing grew more vehement to fully get at the rapturous Center as the highest desirable good. All beings of the space beyond recognize that as clearly, like all of us perceive the common world around us with the same senses. Since the movement went

spiral-wise, the speed of approaching increased constantly. But at some point of the track I was suddenly held back. The movement came to a halt, yes went backwards, so that I moved outward again and withdrew from the yearned-for Center. . . . This backward movement was as smarting to me as approaching had sent me in raptures, and in effect the pain which increased with the growing distance consisted herein that I had to take leave of the good I had recognized as the profoundest possible happiness.

This was why he kept repeating over and over again the word "terrible," after coming out of the anesthesia. Thereafter, his emotional life was marked by this "homesickness" for the Light, this Sun he was to identify as God. It is the bitter pain of homesickness people feel after receiving the grace of a very intimate contact with God; but in a more subtle way, not consciously recognized for what it is, it works in each human soul. This notion of homesickness is no doubt also a good designation for the longing for God of the soul in Purgatory.

* * *

In these near-death accounts, what would have been the next steps, if the experience had not been broken off and the person had not stopped on the threshold of death? Interestingly, there are several accounts of communications by souls from Purgatory that correspond to profound near-death experiences, like the one described by Hellmut Laun, and give an impression of what happens beyond them.

We shall cite two such trustworthy communications. The first comes from a deceased priest who appeared numerous times to the German princess, Eugenie von der Leyen (1867–1929), a woman who was visited in great numbers by the poor souls, begging for her aid, for holy Masses, prayers, mortifications, and other suffrages of the Catholic Church. It is evident that some persons, motivated by pity and mercy, are called to a hard life of self-denial in the service of the suffering souls. Eugenie was one of them. An emotionally stable, amiable, cheerful, and realistic woman, she shared with other privileged helpers of the poor souls the characteristic that she preferred to keep silent about her contacts with these souls; if she hadn't been ordered by her spiritual director to keep a diary on her experiences, they would have fallen into oblivion.

Experiences such as the ones she describes, strange and perhaps incredible as they may appear when one takes cognizance of them for the first time, are of course not run-of-the-mill events. On the other hand, they are less rare than one might think. Many Catholic publications testify to the reality of such apparitions both in the past and the present, but although they are on the whole at least as well documented and often much more informative than the kind of manifestations of the dead reported in the parapsychological literature, they are largely ignored outside the Catholic world. It is the same in the field of miracles: if the "paranormal" points to "religion," in particular, the Catholic religion, you should not take it seriously!

Aside from that, regarding reports (parapsychological and other) about manifestations of the dead, we must critically distinguish between real and pseudo-communications, real and pseudo-apparitions. The latter is the case, for example, with *spiritualist* phenomena. These two fundamentally different categories are often confused in the "scientific" parapsychological literature.

Eugenie von der Leyen reports the apparitions of the soul of a Dominican priest who informed her about the events right after death. When this soul first appeared, on September 5, 1925,[4] his "face was still wholly unrecognizable, a grey lump. He is rather quiet, but mutters incomprehensible words, it seems Latin."

Eugenie continues in her journal,

> *September, 10.* The Dominican is not frightening, but very often around.
> *September, 13.* The Dominican is a Father I have known well, a Frenchman. Was a long time with me, nodded assent when I started praying.
> *September, 17.* I was very sad about something this night and cried. Then a hand was laid on my head. I looked up, it was the Dominican. He said: "Why do you weep?" I: "Because I am not content with myself." . . . He: "Have confidence and be humble!" I: "How can I help you then?" He: "By mortification." Then he remained for a long time. Is not scary at all. It is the first apparition

that began talking unasked for" [Typically, ghosts, i.e., souls from purgatory, seem to wait humbly until their host questions them.]

On September 27 the priest gives the information we are interested in here:

> He was there for long time. I: "Please tell me if we contemplate Our Lord at death at once." He: "Yes, an awful shivering of the soul in adoration and then sinking away in the Purification." I: "Aren't you allowed to say more to me?" He: "No. The more you love God, the greater the beatitude, act according to that!"

He appeared to her for a few months; she to speed up his purification with her prayers and mortifications, and he to give her some priestly advice. In contrast with so many frightening apparitions of souls from Purgatory, Eugenie noted that "I am not at all afraid of the Dominican, I rather enjoy his coming." Although still in Purgatory, this soul could tell her, on November 2, "I am doing fine."

The point the Dominican makes is that the soul of the deceased indeed arrives at its destination, the Light, God: "an awful shivering of the soul in adoration." That is apparently the moment of truth; in the face of the eternal Light and the infinite Purity, the soul understands her imperfections and gravitates to the place or state of purification. It seems to be a spontaneous, natural movement: "then sinking away in the Purification."

∗　∗　∗

Our second illustration of what is to come beyond the point where the near-death experience stops is taken from the communications of a soul not in Purgatory but in Hell. This is the soul of a young woman from Munich, who, after dying in a car accident in 1937, appeared to a girlfriend who was a novice in a monastery.[5] The deceased told her former friend to stop praying for her, as she was in Hell, and gave a startling account of how her way of life and her repeated rejections of the invitations of grace had finally brought her to her terrible destiny. A week after her death, she "wrote" a "letter," which her friend read in a vision that deeply and clearly imprinted itself on her memory:[6]

There, all of a sudden, during our drive home, my husband was blinded by a car from the opposite direction. . . . "Jesses!" it went through me. Not as a prayer, only as a scream. A crushing pain pressed me together—in comparison with the present pain, a trifle. Then I was senseless. Curious, that morning, inexplicably, the idea crossed my mind: you might go to Mass once again. It sounded like imploring. Clearly and resolutely my "No" cut off this thread of thinking . . .

As for me, I suddenly woke up from the darkness of the moment of my departure. Saw myself flooded as with a glaring light. It was at the same place where my corpse was laying. It happened like in a theater, when the lights extinguish in one moment; the curtains rustle apart; in a dismal light an unsuspected scene emerges. The scene of my life.

As in a mirror my soul showed itself to me. The graces trampled underfoot since my childhood, until the last No against God. I felt like a murderer to whom his inanimate victim is presented during the trial.[7] Repent? Never! Be ashamed? Never! But any less could I endure it being under the eyes of the God I had rejected. So only one thing was left: to flee. Like Cain fled from the corpse of Abel, so my soul tore itself away from this horrific sight.

That was the Particular Judgment! The invisible Judge spoke: be gone!

There my soul went down like a sulfuric-yellow shadow to the abode of eternal torment.

With her "last No against God," she entered eternity. "If the tree fall to the south, or to the north, in what place so ever it shall fall, there shall it be," says the Bible.[8] Awakening in a new light, seeing her own (dead) body, a vision of her whole life from the viewpoint of good and evil: these are familiar elements in near-death experiences. But a step further is her definitive conclusion, apparently reached in the presence of God, Who in this case is not adored and intensely desired but hated. The flight from God, down to Hell, is as spontaneous a movement of the soul as the "sinking away" into Purgatory in the case of the Dominican priest. Although in the immaterial "space" hereafter, there is no up and down, both movements away from God are experienced as falling movements, seemingly caused by the soul's weight of sin and its effects.

St. Faustina Kowalska (1905–1938) relates in her *Diary* her mystical experience of the complete moral self-insight that one day will be revealed to every man at the particular judgment after death:[9]

> Once I was summoned to the judgment [seat] of God. I stood alone before the Lord. Jesus appeared such as we know Him during His Passion . . . Suddenly I saw the complete condition of my soul as God sees it. I could clearly see all that is displeasing to God. I did not know that even the smallest transgressions will have to be accounted for. What a moment! Who can describe it? To stand before the Thrice-Holy God! Jesus asked me, "Who are you?" I answered, "I am Your servant, Lord." "You are guilty of one day of fire in purgatory." I wanted to throw myself immediately into the flames of purgatory, but Jesus stopped me.

St. Faustina transmits the awfulness of the soul's confrontation with the Eternal, its insight that perfect holiness is required before it can enjoy God's presence—the smallest imperfections having more weight than even a pure soul as Faustina's had been aware—and the instinctive impulse of the soul to be cleansed, even in the flames of Purgatory.

These examples give at least some impression of the crucial moment when the soul has to render an account of its whole life in the face of God. That is the awful hour of truth: salvation—with or without Purgatory (the latter seems more rare)—or damnation. One of the main reasons for the occasional apparitions of souls from the dead is undoubtedly to urge the living to draw their consequences from this reality.

The basilica at Fatima. The Blessed Virgin reminds the pilgrim of her call to pray the Rosary.

CHAPTER 2

PURGATORY'S PAINS AND JOYS

*I*n her memoirs of the apparitions of Our Lady in Fatima, the eldest seer, Sister Lucia, relates how the subject of Purgatory came up immediately in the first apparition on May 13, 1917. That happened quite naturally, for when the three children—Lucia, Francisco, and Jacinta (ten, almost nine, and seven years old, respectively)— suddenly beheld the beautiful Lady before them on a holm oak, "all dressed in white" and "more brilliant than the sun," while they were "bathed in the light that surrounded her, or rather, which radiated from her," the first question Lucia asked her was, "Where are you from?" And she replied, "I am from Heaven."[1]

"I felt a great inner joy that filled me with confidence and love," Lucia wrote, and "encouraged by the confidence the Lady inspired in me, I asked: 'Shall I go to Heaven too?' Whereupon the Lady answered: 'Yes, you will.' The joy I felt is indescribable"[2]

Lucia went on: "And Jacinta?"

"She will go also."

"And Francisco?"

"He will go there too, but he must say many Rosaries."

And at this point it was normal that the ten-year-old girl would remember two girls from the village who had recently died and whose death must have deeply impressed her:

"They were friends of mine and used to come to my home to learn weaving with my eldest sister. Is Maria das Neves in Heaven?"

"Yes, she is."

"And Amélia?"

"She will be in purgatory until the end of the world" (Lucia added in her *Fourth Memoir* that she seemed to be "between eighteen and twenty years of age").

Maria das Neves is already in Heaven, thanks be to God! Not all persons go to Purgatory or have to be there for a long period of time—that is a relief! But Amélia: until the end of the world!? Surely, a startling and perplexing communication! Some commentators have tried to tone it down, but not Lucia herself. In her last booklet, which she wrote not long before her death, she shares her ideas about the shocking remark of Our Lady with respect to Amélia's time in Purgatory. After her long life of meditation and devotedness to the message of Fatima, Lucia offers an original reflection, which may serve well as an introduction to the mystery of Purgatory:

> I have been asked many questions concerning this reply of Our Lady and I don't know too well how to answer them. I didn't ask Our Lady for a clarification, I was too young to think about that. But I have meditated a lot about this detail of the Message.
>
> After all—I ask myself—what is purgatory, actually? . . . We see that the word "purgatory" means "purification," and as all of us are more or less sinners, all of us need being purified of our own sins, faults, and imperfections, in order to be admitted to the enjoyment of the possession of the Kingdom of eternal glory.
>
> We can still realize this purification during this life, if God gives us the time for it: by asking God for forgiveness, with sincere repentance and the resolution to change our life by doing penance, receiving the sacrament of confession.

Here, Sister Lucia sums up all kinds of sins and continues,

All these things, and many others, too numerous to mention, are against the commandments of the Law of God and require a great purification, even if they have already been confessed and forgiven with respect to their punishment . . . but not expiated with respect to their purification; until this [expiation] renders us worthy to be admitted to the immense ocean of God's Being.

This purification—that is called "Purgatory"—can be more or less extended, depending on the number of our sins, faults, and imperfections, and on their gravity, for which we have not given complete satisfaction by means of reparation, good works, penance, and prayers.

And how are we purified in Purgatory, or what purifies us? I don't know very well. In the past, they said that we are purified by being thrown in a hot fire, and that this fire was equal to that of Hell. Modern writers seem not to concord any more with this way of thinking.

As for me, it seems to me that what purifies us is love, the fire of divine love, which is communicated by God to the souls in proportion as every soul corresponds. It is said that if a soul is granted the grace to die with a perfect act of love, that this love purifies it totally, so that it can go straight to Heaven. This shows us that what purifies is love, along with contrition, sorrow for having offended God and the neighbor, by sins, faults, and imperfections, because all this is against the first and last commandments of the Law of God: *You shall love the Lord thy God with thy whole heart, and with thy whole soul, and with thy whole strength.* That way, the small or big flame of love—even though it be only a wick that is still smoldering—will not extinguish, but will be scintillating and increasing until it totally purifies the soul and makes it dignified to be admitted, to live in the immense ocean of the Being of God, to participate with all the other blessed ones in the wisdom, power, knowledge, and love of God, in proportion as God wants to communicate it to every soul; while all united sing the hymn of eternal love, praising and glorifying our God, Creator and Savior.

I don't know if all I am saying here is exactly so; if Holy Church says it in another way, believe her and not me, who am poor and

ignorant; I can be mistaken. This is what I think and not what I
know . . . Thus we see that our purgatory can be more or less prolonged, conform the state of grace and the degree of love of God
we find ourselves in at the moment of passing from earthly life to
the sphere of supernatural life, from time to eternity.[3]

It is not what I know, but what I think, the sister writes prudently.
Nevertheless, what she *thinks* may help to lift a little corner of the veil
that hangs over the mystery of Purgatory. It is, moreover, very much
akin to the explanation given by that great mystic, the "theologian
of purgatory,"[4] Catherine of Genoa. These and similar reflections are
but approximations of the supernatural reality, nevertheless they cast
at least some rays of light on it.

Sister Lucia surmises that the intensity of the love of God, with
which the soul crosses the threshold into eternity—along with the
weight of sins not atoned for—determines the duration of the process of purification. Therefore, the fire of Purgatory is individual,
person-bound, and does not equally affect all souls. Lucia doesn't
say that a wavering candle flame of love of God, so to speak, whose
weakness would immensely prolong the soul's purification, is not
painful. It is true that according to certain communications of souls
from Purgatory, not all souls are suffering terribly all the time, but
there seems to be little doubt that, as a rule, this suffering is beyond
our imagination. But then, it is also beyond our imagination that the
purifying power of a person's love of God can cause such consuming
pain and distress.

Maybe we understand this reality a bit more when we realize that
the "naked" soul in Purgatory has nothing earthly any more to attach
itself to or to strive after and that its encounter with God right after
death has wounded it with an intense pining for Him, whom it has
for a fleeting moment recognized as the ultimate fulfillment of all its
longings, wishes, and hopes, of its craving for happiness. Sister Lucia
seems to imply that this pining is less intense in souls with little love
of God at the point of death—the more love, the deeper the unhap-
piness in the absence of the beloved. Nonetheless, once having seen

Him, the torment of being far from Him surpasses any feeling of being banished from the beloved things one knew on earth.

Recalling the near-death experience of Hellmut Laun, whose yearning after the Center of bliss intensified the nearer he came to It, one might suppose that the soul with this small flame of love does not pine so much because it is still far from Him. Less pining would amount to being less purified by the flames of longing.

Lucia's notion of the purifying mystical "fire of divine love," which she thinks is proportioned to the soul's own love of God, doesn't exclude the possibility that it burns like some earthly fire. After all, the sensation of pain by burning is perceived by the soul, by human consciousness. On earth, that pain arises from the soul's perception of nervous and brain stimulations, but why couldn't the very same sensation be provoked directly in the soul by the nonmaterial stimulus of an "emotional state" or awareness? Change to, "It could be even more intense, in fact, because the protective reaction of falling unconscious at high levels of pain does not exist anymore. Also, on earth, immaterial motions of the soul may produce sensations similar to physical burning: desires can burn, love may set a heart aflame, and the like. It therefore needs not make much difference if the fire of Purgatory is to be conceived as material or immaterial: the experience is the same.[5]

The fires of purification and Hell, says St. Thomas Aquinas, act "not by a natural movement, but as instruments of the divine Justice, which is, as it were, the fire of these fires and endow them with a force which they intrinsically do not have."[6] God's justice and his mercy are two essential elements of his Substance and so intertwined that where His Justice operates, His Mercy is also at work. The explanation of Sister Lucia mitigates the frightening aspect of God's infinite justice, subordinating it as it were to His love. That way, Purgatory gets a more comforting, more "humane" aspect so as to make it more acceptable to our feelings. God appears as the loving Father who cannot but cleanse his impure child precisely because He wants to make it unimaginably happy. The image of a relentless, cruel Punisher evaporates in this vision of the fire of love of God that He himself enkindles in the soul. (This does not apply to Hell, though.)

In accordance with this view, many souls from Purgatory have affirmed what seems at first glance completely incomprehensible: that the soul after death is eager to go to Purgatory, because after seeing God, it longs for its perfect purity, for giving full satisfaction to God, and that it suffers with increasing contentment and love of God.

CHAPTER 3

HOLY SOUL, OR DEMONIC IMPOSTOR?

*M*any Protestants—not all of them, for sure—are inclined to take all apparitions of the dead as demonic, or at least to disbelieve or disregard them. Indeed, the frightening and ghastly impression they make, plus the fact that they are sometimes accompanied with or preceded by poltergeist phenomena, may suggest activities of the devil. Some apparitions that present themselves as souls of the dead may indeed turn out to be demons in disguise, seeking to deceive the credulous. That is true for all so-called manifestations of the dead during states of trance, hypnosis, or at spiritualist and other magic or occult sessions: they are by no means the departed persons they pretend to be, but hoaxes or demonic imposters.

On the other hand, damned human souls from Hell, who manifest themselves very rarely, should not be mistaken for "demons." Souls from Purgatory and Hell have one decisive point in common: they cannot be conjured up at will.[1]

After the death of a beloved person, some desperate and naive people feel tempted to make use of spiritualist mediums in order, they credulously assume, to get contact with the deceased. In reality, when there is a supernatural phenomenon in which the deceased seems to manifest himself, it is invariably demonic deception.

* * *

Father Delaporte[2] relates striking "facts which occurred at Rauzan [Gironde, France] in 1853." The Viscount de Meslon, investigating spiritualist phenomena, questioned a spirit that manifested itself by the intermediary of a round "speaking table."[3] The spirit claimed to be his brother, who had died a pious death in 1845. The spirit answered "with the utmost precision all the questions put to him," so seemed very trustworthy. Then the spirit was

> adjured, *in the name of the living God*, not to deceive, and cruci-
> fixes and blessed objects are placed on the table. The spirit per-
> sists in saying that he was sent by God to enlighten his family, to
> defend it against the snares of the devils, and to guide in the way
> of virtue and truth. Every moment he quotes . . . sentences from
> Holy Writ, urges his hearers to love God and to honor the blessed
> Virgin. When asked questions relating to financial matters, or the
> future, he strenuously refuses to answer and admonishes, in the
> name of God, those who interrogate him, as to their lightness and
> imprudence.
>
> But, one evening, a small work-table, questioned in its turn,
> advises distrust of the spirit of the round table. The latter replies
> by summoning, *in the name of the living God*, the spirit of the
> work-table to confess that he is the spirit of evil. After an obsti-
> nate resistance and some fearful contortions, the little table avows
> that he is animated by the Devil, envious of the good which the
> departed soul was doing to his family. "Thenceforward," says
> Mr. de Meslon, "our confidence would have been absolute, when
> God . . . would have no longer permitted the devil to deceive us."
>
> One Sunday, the little round table, which almost always spoke
> of itself, at first refused to answer, then rose up impatiently, and
> said to us these words *verbatim*: "I am tired repeating to you inces-
> santly honeyed words which I do not think, and expressing to
> you affectionate sentiments, when I have no feeling for you but
> hatred."

"But are you not him whom you pretend to be?"

"No."

"Who are you, then?"

"The spirit of evil."

"What was the objective of the disgraceful farce you have been so long playing with us?"

"Seeking to inspire you with confidence, the better to deceive you afterwards."

"You hate us, then?"

"Yes, because you are Christians."

Then the spirit took leave of us with these words: "God *forces* me to speak thus; hell claims me back; farewell."

✳︎   ✳︎   ✳︎

This is an older example. In a more recent one, English-Canadian investigative journalist Joe Fisher reached the same conclusion.[4] Convinced at first of the reality of the "spirit guides" that talked to several persons, including himself, during spiritualist sessions (the New Age practice of "channeling"), he nevertheless wanted to check their "information" about events that allegedly had happened in Europe and North America. Gradually it dawned upon him that something was amiss, and in the end he had to unmask all such spirits as most dangerous liars, bent on the total physical and psychic destruction of their "protégés." Not a Christian, Fisher designated them by the Tibetan notion of "hungry ghosts": spirits that supposedly feed on the lives of their deceived victims. The Christian would simply call them "demons," as the devil is characterized by Our Lord by exactly these two activities: lying and murdering.

Since many people, including many Catholics, are not free from superstition and sometimes do not resist the wishful expectation that some or other spiritualist medium will bring them in contact with the dead, it is not superfluous to repeat that all ghosts of spiritualism are always demonic frauds. A well-known investigator of parapsychological phenomena in the early 20th century, Godfrey Raupert, whose experiments with spiritualists led him to a firm belief in the devil, emphasized the dangers involved in mistaking such spirits for souls of the departed. The naive person who does not know that the

devil is able to appear as "an angel of light"—yes, even as Christ or
the Blessed Virgin, as witnessed in the lives of many saints—is an
easy prey for him.

Raupert was involved in the story of an intelligent but naive English priest, the proper secretary of the archbishop of Westminster,
Cardinal Vaughan. The secretary attended spiritualist sessions at the
house of a general, shortly after the death of his chief, the cardinal:

> To the boundless astonishment of the young clergyman, very
> soon a fully materialized figure came to the fore from the back-
> ground of the curtain, that bore the form and facial features of
> the deceased Cardinal, pulled straight to him and whispered more
> or less the following in his ear: "I have an important statement to
> make. What I taught in my earthly life is not true. I recognized
> that immediately at my entrance into the world where I am liv-
> ing now. You must tell everyone that you have talked to me and
> what you have been told." After words of this tenet the phantom
> disappeared.

The "cardinal" reappeared in a number of subsequent sessions,
and, according to the young monsignor, "answered all questions in
such a manner as to leave him no doubt that he had to do with
the deceased Cardinal. And with that came for him the total col-
lapse of his Catholic faith." The young monsignor left the priesthood
and became a "convinced spiritualist." It was only years later that
he woke up to reality and learned to see through the deception and
dangers of these diabolical apparitions.[5]

* * *

One can understand those Protestants who, on account of such
deceptive apparitions, disbelieve in the existence of real apparitions
of the dead, be they from Purgatory or Hell (especially from Purgatory, because many Protestants do not believe in a place or state of
atonement after death). They presume that all alleged apparitions
of the dead must be demonic fakes.[6] However, that extreme view is
as untenable as the uncritical belief in the authenticity of all ghosts
that pretend to be spirits of the dead. There is an impressive body of

well-documented evidence of apparitions or manifestations of souls from Purgatory, even well-documented evidence of apparitions of souls of Protestants, with Protestants as witnesses.[7]

The curious history of the renowned Lutheran minister Johann Christoph Blumhardt, who had dealings with the spirits or ghosts appearing in the house of the pious Protestant woman Gottliebin Dittus during 1842 and 1843 in the small German village of Möttlingen, has become notorious in Protestant circles.[8] It is difficult to disentangle what exactly was going on in this complicated history, in part because Blumhardt's information is far from complete; but as much is clear that some of the spirits were indeed demonic, others no doubt souls from Purgatory who seemed under the sway of demons (probably in punishment for their engagement in occult practices during their life). Of interest to us here, however, is that for all his dogmatic rejection of Purgatory and his refusal to pray for the latter type of spirits, Blumhardt felt the necessity to identify them as a distinct category of "demons"—as he indiscriminately called all apparitions—and that he discovered that they called for special, merciful treatment. These spirits seemed not irretrievably damned and were characterized not only by grievous suffering but also by their insistent, heart-rendering demands for help:

> Furthermore, I report something about the demons [*sic*] from that time that yearned for deliverance. For a long time, I did not listen to their talking and often came under great pressure when I saw the sorrowful expression, the supplicating raised hands and the torrents of tears flowing from the eyes, and moreover heard sounds and sighs of anguish, desperation, and supplication that would have softened a stone. Therefore, much as I braced myself not to comply with any manner intended to release them, since with everything that took place my first thought was of some dangerous and baneful devilish deception, and since I feared for the soberness of my evangelical faith, yet in the end I could not get away with it without making an experiment, especially while precisely these demons, who seemed to have some hope for themselves, could not be induced to go away, neither by threats nor by exhortations.

The first "demon" who made him venture to show a little bit of mercy was a woman he had known well when she was alive. She "exclaimed unwaveringly and resolutely that she wanted to belong to the Savior, not to the devil . . . Then she urgently implored me to pray for her . . . Now my heart was breaking on account of her." Moved by pity, he took a small, "risky" step. The woman had asked him permission to stay in his (Lutheran) church, and he agreed, "provided Jesus gives his permission," whereupon the spirit seemed content and vanished.

In this connection, we remember that some poor souls (possibly also some damned souls) have to stay on earth for some period of time. Reports of poor souls dwelling in churches are not exceptional; these souls seem to get more "rest" in holy places and places of prayer than somewhere else. Thus Blumhardt continues, "In the same way, other spirits . . . who otherwise seemed to have love of the Savior, sought liberation and safety. Only with utter carefulness and pertinent prayers to the Lord did I venture into what I could not refuse. My slogan was always: 'When Jesus permits it!'"

His courage and good-heartedness—if he had rigidly stuck to the principle that all apparitions are demonic, it would have been easier for him to leave these clinging, begging spirits alone—urged him to act. Had he ventured some more steps in this direction, by openly praying for them and visibly improving their condition, he would possibly have lost all reservations concerning Purgatory.

In this case we see yet another clear distinction between demonic apparitions and those of the poor souls. Demons do not unshakably persist in professing that they want to belong to Jesus alone, they do not consistently beg and implore for help and prayers, and do not move to compassion. Poor souls, on the other hand, are not sensitive to adjurations and commands to vanish in the Name of God, in the Name of Jesus. Indeed, their anxious begging for help signals hope for deliverance.

CHAPTER 4

APPARITIONS OF DAMNED SOULS

*H*uman souls from Hell are not easily mistaken for souls from Purgatory. Just as with demons, they do not sadly beg for prayers, help, and compassion; nor do they show the slightest sign of hope. According to St. Augustine, apparitions of souls of the damned are very rare, but "still one can suppose that they sometimes appear, as an example to the living and to inculcate fear in them."[1] We may speculate that God does not order many such apparitions for the same reason why, in Our Lord's parable of the poor Lazarus, Abraham declined the request of the merciless rich man in Hell to send Lazarus to warn his like-minded brothers: "If they do not hear Moses and the prophets, neither will they be convinced if some one should rise from the dead."[2]

Everyone can see the realism of this reply of Abraham. Many people who "do not hear Moses and the prophets," who are not open-minded and intent on seeking the truth, who out of lack of humility or lust of ease are unwilling to hear about God, faith, or the demands of objective, transcendent morality, will shrug their shoulders before any supernatural manifestation, however impressive and trustworthy it may be. What they do not want to exist, for them, does not exist.

But the open-minded, who judges with sober realism, will learn from well-evidenced apparitions. They can cause him to meditate on realities he perhaps had no inkling of before; they can strengthen his faith in the supernatural; and they can serve as a warning, because they dramatically emphasize the consequences of man's present moral choices for all eternity. In this sense, all apparitions of the dead are educational. They are graces from Heaven that can be accepted or rejected. That is true for apparitions from Heaven, Purgatory, and Hell alike.

Msgr. de Ségur, then Bishop of Saint-Denis (Paris), recounts in his small book *Hell* (1876) several well-documented instances of apparitions of damned souls. We reproduce two of them, which had occurred shortly before the booklet was written.[3]

> The first took place almost in my family. It was in Russia, in Moscow, a short time before the horrible campaign of 1812. My maternal grandfather, Count Rostopchine, the military governor of Moscow, was very intimate with General Count Orloff, famous for his bravery, but as godless as he was brave.
>
> One day, after a fine supper sprinkled with abundant drinks, Count Orloff and one of his friends, General V., also a Voltairian,[4] had engaged in terribly ridiculing Religion and especially hell. "And if, by coincidence," said Orloff, "if by coincidence something would exist on the other side of the curtain?" "Okay!" replied General V., "whichever of the two of us who shall depart first will come back to give word of it to the other one. Is that agreed?" "Excellent idea!" answered Count Orloff, and both of them, although half-drunk, gave each other their word of honor, that they would not fail their commitment.
>
> Some weeks later, one of those great wars such as Napoleon had the gift to stir up at that time burst out; the Russian army started a campaign, and General V. received orders to leave immediately in order to take an important command.
>
> He had left Moscow for two or three weeks, when one morning, very early in the morning, while my grandfather was dressing, the door of his room is brusquely opened. It was Count Orloff, in

dressing gown and slippers, his hair on end, with wild eyes, deadly pale. "What! Orloff, is it you? At this hour? And in this clothes? What is the matter with you? What happened?"

"My dear," answers Count Orloff, "I believe that I am becoming mad. I just saw General V." "General V.? Did he come back, then?" "Well, no," continues Orloff, throwing himself on a sofa and holding his head in his two hands, "No, he has not come back! And that is what frightens me!"

My grandfather did not understand anything of it. He tried to soothe him. "Tell me then," he said to him, "what has happened to you and what all of this is supposed to mean." Then, making an effort to contain his emotions, Count Orloff related the following:

"My dear Rostopchine, some time ago, V. and I swore mutually that the first of us who died would come and tell the other one if there is something on the other side of the curtain. Well, this morning, hardly half an hour ago, I was calmly in my bed, awake for a long time, not thinking of my friend at all, when suddenly the two curtains of my bed were brusquely parted, and I see, at two steps from me, General V., standing upright, pale, his right hand on his chest, and saying to me: 'There is a hell and I am there!,' and he disappeared. I came to you at once. My head is splitting apart! What a strange thing! I do not know what to think about it!"

My grandfather calmed him down as best he could. That was not easy. He spoke of hallucinations, nightmares; perhaps he had been asleep. There are so many extraordinary, inexplicable things; and other trivialities of that sort that are the consolation of free-thinkers. Then he had his horses put to the carriage and let Count Orloff bring him back to his hotel.

Now, ten or twelve days after this strange incident, an army messenger brought my grandfather, among other news, that of the death of General V. The very morning of the day Count Orloff had seen and heard him, at the same hour he had appeared to him in Moscow, the unfortunate general, sallied to reconnoiter the position of the enemy, had been shot through his breast by a bullet and had fallen stark dead!

"There is a hell, and I am there!" These are the words of someone who "came back."

When Msgr. de Ségur told this story in 1859 to "a very distinguished priest, the Superior of an important [religious] community," the latter thought it was not so amazing after all, because there were more "facts of that sort." And he told the bishop an experience he learned

from a certain source, two or three years ago, from a very near relative of the person to whom it happened. The moment I am talking to you [Christmas 1859], this lady is still alive; she is a little over forty years.

She was in London, the winter of 1847 to 1848. She was a widow, about twenty-nine years old, very worldly, very rich, and very good-looking. Among the gallants who frequented her salon was noted a young lord, whose assiduities compromised her in particular and whose behavior was otherwise anything but edifying.

One evening, or rather one night (for it was already past midnight), she was reading in her bed I don't know what novel, waiting for sleep to come. It struck one hour by her clock; she blew out her taper. She was about to fall asleep when, to her great astonishment, she noticed that a wan, strange glimmer of light, which seemed to come from the door of the salon, spread gradually in her room and increased from one moment to the other. Stupefied, she put her eyes wide open, not knowing what this could mean. She got frightened when she saw the door slowly open and the young lord, the accomplice in her disorders, enter her room. Before she could have said a single word to him, he was near her, seized her left arm at the wrist, and said to her in English, in a striding voice: "There is a hell!" The pain she felt in her arm was so great that she lost her senses.

When she came to again, half an hour later, she rang for her chambermaid. On entering, she smelled a strong smell of burning; when she approached her mistress, who could hardly speak, she noticed on her wrist a burn so deep that the bone was laid bare and the flesh nearly consumed; this burn was the size of a man's hand. Moreover, she remarked that the carpet from the door of the salon to the bed, and from the bed to this same door, bore the imprint of a man's steps, which had burned the tissue through and through. On the order of her mistress, she opened the door of the salon. More traces on the carpet.

The next day the unhappy lady learned, with a terror that is easy to imagine, that on that very night, close upon one o'clock in the morning, her lord had been found dead-drunk under the table, that his servants had carried him to his room and that he had died in their arms.

I don't know if this terrible lesson has converted the unfortunate lady once and for all; but what I know is that she is still alive; only, that in order to keep out of sight the traces of her sinister burn she wears on her left wrist, as if it were a bracelet, a broad gold band, which she does not take off day or night.

I repeat, I have all these details from her near relative, a serious Christian, whose word I give the fullest credit. In the family itself, they are never spoken of; and I myself confide them to you, suppressing every proper name.

The story of the lady with the "bracelet" is of some special interest for us, as it exemplifies that not only souls from Purgatory but also souls from Hell may leave visible marks—in this case, the serious burn on her wrist and the burns in the carpet—which evidence the fierce fire in which they are immersed.[5]

CHAPTER 5

EVIDENCE FOR PURGATORY IN
EARLY CHRISTIAN HISTORY

Notions of Heaven and Hell are universal and go back to pre-
historic times. There are many indications that this is also true
for the idea of a "middle state" where the soul that does not deserve
Hell but is not good enough for Heaven must be purified or do penance before entering eternal bliss.

The widespread age-old belief in reincarnation or migration of the
souls (into newborns or even animals) was perhaps a degeneration
of an originally more correct insight; at any rate, it contained the
wisdom of the necessity of some purification after death.[1] Modern
Western man is not used to seeing things that way, imbued as he
is with the prejudice—the "scientistic" myth—of a gradual upward
evolution of everything, including the essential notions relating to
being and existence, such as the notion of one God, of Heaven, and
Hell. The real development may as well have been quite the reverse;
original insights may have been obscured in the course of time by
fantasies, wrong understanding, and man's tendency to superstition.[2]

The description of the next world in the writings of the Greek philosopher Plato (about 400 years before Christ) certainly reflects a very old conception: those who have lived very piously go straight to a heavenly state, the wicked straight to Hell or Tartarus, and the others to a great lake where they are to atone for their faults until they are absolved.[3] Such ideas seem almost "archetypical"— that is, primal mental representations of a reality that the human psyche, or rather, human moral conscience, somehow knows by instinct: that our wrongdoing must not only be forgiven but also be "made good," expiated. Guilty feelings and the need for penance go together. It is therefore also psychologically probable that mankind has always had the intuition that justice requires a form of penance in the afterlife. Plato's lake is not a lake of fire, but since we have to do with material images for a supernatural reality, this should not be given too much weight.[4]

In Old Testament times, the books of the Maccabees mention the practice of donating money for sacrifices "for the sins of the dead" (who were fallen on the battlefield), and it is said that "it is therefore a holy and wholesome thought to pray for the dead, that they may be loosed from sins."[5] Offering sacrifices for the dead is an extremely old and almost universal custom that at least hints at some awareness of Purgatory, and praying for the dead is so spontaneous and human a reaction that one can hardly believe that this habit originated only a few hundred years before Christ.

The basic Jewish belief in what Catholicism calls Purgatory, as it is apparent from the second book of Maccabees,[6] has not changed very much over the centuries. Even now, the orthodox Jews who accept the Talmud—the traditional explanations of the Mosaic laws or Torah—believe in a period of purification after death (up to a maximum of 12 months). The purification is effected by a suffering that is often described as burning in a fire. The person who has been very wicked cannot be purified and is relegated to eternal Hell. The fire of purification and the fire of Hell are seen as the same, the "Gehinnom." The sons of the departed therefore have the duty to recite the "kaddish" for their deceased parents for one year; this prayer is thought "to help raise the soul to its ultimate destination in God's presence."[7] Another beautiful, traditional Jewish prayer for the dead, beginning with the Hebrew words *El, Malei Rachamim* translates as follows:

> Oh God, full of mercy, who dwells on high, grant perfect rest beneath the sheltering wings of Your presence, among the holy and the pure who shine as the brightness of the sky, to the soul of [the deceased] who has gone to his eternity, and in whose memory charity is offered by [the supplicant]. May his rest be in Paradise. May the Master of Mercy bring him under the cover of His wings, and let his soul be bound up in the bond of life. May the LORD be his inheritance, and may he rest in peace where he lay, and let us say, Amen.[8]

Who will not recognize the great similarity between this prayer and many Catholic prayers in the holy Mass of Requiem for the defunct? *Requiem aeternam, dona ei(s), Domine.* "Lord, give him/her/ them eternal rest," a rest that implies holiness and purity, as the soul must enter the company of the "holy and pure," "under the wings of Your presence," which is Holiness and Purity Itself.

These Jewish beliefs and customs relating to the dead must be very similar to those in the time of Our Lord, and they help us to understand what the first Christians believed. No doubt the early Christians adopted the idea of Purgatory itself, as well as praying for the dead and making sacrifices for them—including offering the Immaculate Sacrifice, holy Mass—from the Jewish mother religion, which Christ had come to perfect.[9] This is likely the simple explanation why the New Testament only makes indirect references to Purgatory: there was no doubt about its existence.

El, Malei Rachamim! We recognize the very words of that prayer for the departed in inscriptions in the catacombs of the first centuries, the cemeteries of the early Roman Christians:

"Eternal light shine upon thee, Timothea, in Christ!"

"Let [the reader] pray to God to take to Himself her spirit holy and pure."

"Thee, o heavenly Father, we implore to have mercy."[10]

Purgatory and charity for the dead must have been an integral part of the Christian faith and practice from the earliest beginnings.

* * *

A moving early Christian account of a manifestation of a "poor soul" can be found in the "Acta" of the martyrdom of St. Perpetua from Carthago, described by the young martyr herself in the year 202 during her stay in the dungeon before she and other Christians were thrown to the wild animals. In a vision she saw her deceased seven-year-old brother, Dinocrates, in a pitiful condition, in a gloomy place "with many others, flushed with heat, and thirsty." There was a basin full of water, but its edge was so high that the boy could not drink.

"Then I awoke and knew that my brother was suffering. But I trusted that I could help him out . . . And I prayed day and night for Dinocates, with sighs and tears, that he be given to me." Then St. Perpetua got a second vision and saw her little brother, healthy, freshly washed, and playing cheerfully. The basin had lowered, and he could drink as much as he wanted. "Then I awoke and knew that my brother's punishment was over."[11]

The meaning of these symbolic visions is not abstruse. The water that the boy and the other thirsty souls longed for is the water of eternal life Our Lord indicated when He spoke to the Samaritan woman, the water that quenches man's thirst forever. The boy is thirsty for God. Before he was allowed to drink, he had to be "cleansed" and "cured," purified from whatever remnants of sin even a boy of seven years may take with him into the next world. The supplications of his generous and courageous sister must have considerably accelerated the cleansing process.

CHAPTER 6

THE CHURCH FATHERS
AND LATER SAINTS ON PURGATORY

*T*he notion of Purgatory and the belief that the living can come to the aid of the suffering souls there are anything but medieval inventions. Affirmations of the ancient Church Fathers show that the apostles themselves professed them. St. John Chrysostom, bishop of Constantinople around the year 400, said that the apostles ordained the commemoration of the departed during holy Mass, as it is a great help for them.[1] "As we have learned from the apostles, praying for the dead is helpful to them," preached St. Augustine (354–430), who preached and wrote a great deal on Purgatory and the means to help the poor souls.[2] His small work *The Care Due to the Dead* is a classic.[3]

Augustine's spiritual father, St. Ambrose, bishop of Milan (from 374–397), said that the souls in Purgatory pray for *us* so that we may recognize our sins and that what we do for them will be rewarded a hundredfold.[4] The existence of Purgatory was denied by some followers of the heretic Arians and by the Gnostics, but the Council of Carthage in 411 recommended prayers for the dead.

St. Thomas Aquinas (1225–1274), to whom his deceased sister had appeared from Purgatory to implore his spiritual help, emphasized in line with the ancient Fathers the exceptional value of the Sacrifice of holy Mass for the release of the holy souls.[5] Interestingly, he inferred from several trustworthy apparitions that some souls have to undergo their purification on *earth*, probably as an example for the living and to urge the living not to forget them.[6] This may account for the universally known phenomenon of recurrent apparitions of departed persons on certain fixed places (e.g., the place where they lived) or the site of their sins.

Very many canonized saints in Catholic history had frequent contacts with souls from Purgatory and were their great helpers through their prayers and sacrifices. This is logical enough when we realize that helping the suffering souls is an important form of charity.[7] Of St. Gertrude of Helfta in Saxony (1256–1302), it is known that she released many souls from Purgatory by her "suffrages," especially by offering holy Communion for them. One day Christ Himself affirmed the particular efficacy of the efforts of saintly persons like her when He said that "it would not be in opposition to my justice to release them [the souls] immediately, if you would confidently pray for this purpose."[8]

This may be a reason why it is usually pure, pious souls whom the suffering souls are allowed to visit to ask for relief. Among them, we find St. Margaret Mary Alacoque (1647–1690), whose calling it was to spread the devotion to the Sacred Heart of Jesus; it is no coincidence that this devotion was, from the beginning, intimately united to the devotion to the souls in Purgatory.[9] Thus the connection of the devotion to the poor souls with the devotion to the Sacred Heart, as manifested in the church on the Lungotevere in Rome with its *Museo del Purgatorio*, is rooted in a venerable tradition. The church points to the mystery of the perfect merging of the Justice of the God-Man with his Mercy in the infinite depths of his divine-human Heart.

Blessed Catherine Emmerick (1774–1824), the Westphalian nun who was gifted with so many visions of the life and Passion of Our Lord, was also a visionary of Purgatory. She got fascinating insights into the condition of the poor souls whom she generously assisted. In step with an old tradition, she was convinced that these souls "receive no *direct* aid from heaven; everything they obtain comes from the faithful who live in this world."[10]

✳   ✳   ✳

Insofar as they lent themselves to verification and have been checked, communications from Purgatory have invariably proven veracious—in contrast to the affirmations of the "lying ghosts" of spiritualism. There are numerous cases like that of the venerable Sister Josepha Menéndez (1885–1923) of the Congregation of the Sacred Heart in Poitiers, France. For each of the many souls unknown to her who humbly implored her intercession and sacrifices, she wrote down the name, date, and place of their death, data that could always be substantiated.[11]

It is furthermore remarkable that the reports of apparitions of souls from Purgatory are highly consistent in the course of the centuries and vary but little from one historical period to another. Purgatory has always been represented as a fierce fire, a burning away of all stains of the soul, regardless of the century or cultural period the apparition took place. And there is always proof of a twofold suffering: namely the "pain of loss," which is the soul's painful longing for God, and the "pain of sense," which is felt as if the bodily senses were still intact.[12] For example, the account given in the 20th century by Sister Faustina of her mystical visit to Purgatory does not really differ from similar accounts given many centuries earlier (e.g., accounts from her 17th-century compatriot, the Blessed Father Papczynksi, of his visits to Purgatory). Faustina writes in 1926,

> I saw my Guardian Angel, who ordered me to follow him. In a moment I was in a misty place full of fire in which there was a great crowd of suffering souls. They were praying fervently, but without effect for themselves; only we can come to their aid. The flames which were burning them did not touch me at all. My Guardian Angel did not leave me for an instant. I asked these souls what their greatest suffering was. They answered me in one voice that their greatest torment was longing for God. . . . [I heard an interior voice] which said, *My mercy does not want this, but justice demands it.* Since that time, I am in closer communion with the suffering souls.[13]

By the way, if the souls in Purgatory cannot pray for themselves, what are they praying for, except that their prayer will also be a prayer of adoration? We mentioned the opinion of the early Church Father St. Ambrose that they pray for the living so that they may recognize their sins. Apparently, their suffering makes them most keenly aware that holiness is by far the most important boon to implore for the ones they love—it means less suffering in Purgatory and a quicker path to eternal bliss. In addition, it appears from many communications of poor souls that they also pray for the *temporal* needs of the living: for their beloved, their family and benefactors, in the first place. Terrestrial bonds of love continue after death.

St. Bridget of Sweden (1303–1373), however, heard the suffering souls nevertheless indirectly supplicating Christ's mercy for *themselves*, asking Him to incite the faithful on earth to come to their aid: "We implore Thee for the sake of Thy infinite mercy to turn away Thine eyes from our innumerable sins . . . Imbue with Thy true love the religious, the priests and the faithful, so that they may hasten to our relief by their prayers, sacrifices, alms deeds and indulgences. They can aid us if they wish; they can hasten our union with Thee, O God!"[14]

Pope John Paul II visits the monastery and sanctuary of Jasna Góra, June 18, 1983.

* * *

Various councils have formulated the Catholic doctrine on Purgatory, but the Council of Trent (from 1545, with a long interruption, to 1562) had to be very articulate, as this article of faith was questioned by the Reformers and even bluntly denied by Calvin, who fell back in this respect into the old Gnostic heresy.

Actually, Trent dogmatized what had been believed all along. First, although the guilt of a penitent sinner may have been forgiven, that does not mean that automatically all his "debt of temporal punishment" is discharged. In short, he may have to do penance in order to be purified, whether in this life or in the next: in Purgatory. Furthermore, the souls in Purgatory "are helped by the suffrages of the faithful, but particularly by the Sacrifice of the Altar."[15]

This doctrine is reiterated in the Catechism of the Catholic Church of 1992, which was composed on the initiative of Pope John Paul II.[16]

CHAPTER 7

THE FIRE OF PURGATORY ACCORDING TO CATHERINE OF GENOA

*T*he mystic St. Catherina of Genoa (1447-1510)

> while still in the flesh . . . experienced the fiery love of God, a love that consumed her, cleansing and purifying all, so that once quitted this life she could appear forthwith in God's presence. As she dwelt on this love, the condition of the souls of the faithful in purgatory, where they are cleansed of the remaining rust and stain of sin, became clear to her. She rejoiced in her union with God in this loving purgatory, and so did the souls in purgatory, she realized, who have no choice but to be there, and this because of God's just decree.[1]

Catherine lived Purgatory in this world, not symbolically, but literally. She tried to put her inner experience in words, although "tongue cannot express nor heart understand the full meaning of purgatory, which the soul willingly accepts as a mercy."[2] In spite of these limitations, her insights into Purgatory, based on her continuous experience of being consumed by an inner purifying fire, are most enlightening. She has been called the "theologian of purgatory"[3]; and St. Francis de Sales (1567–1622), the famous bishop of Geneva, Doctor of the Church and outstanding spiritual counselor, deemed her so-called *Tract* on Purgatory "wonderful and very seraphic" and the product of "pure inspiration and divine enlightenment." (Catherine herself had declared that she had "seen all this in the divine light.") The most important points of his own doctrine on Purgatory are almost literally the same as the affirmations of St. Catherine.[4]

The fire of Purgatory, which comprises the sufferings of the "pain of loss" and the "pain of sense," is the fire of the love of God enkindled in the soul right after death. Then it sees itself and all its "rust of sin"—which St. Catherine specifies as "the lower self in us . . . the inclination to evil . . . the soul's self-centeredness . . . the many hidden flaws . . . [the soul's unpaid] debt"[5]—in the light of God's Presence.

The soul that crossed the threshold to the next life, and is "determined to sin no more," is forgiven by God, thus freed of sin and guilt. Then "it is close to its first creation . . . [so that its] instinct of beatitude asserts itself with such impetus and fiery charity that any impediment becomes unbearable." Instinct of beatitude! This psychic instinct, "weakened by original sin," is the soul's inborn longing for purity, for infinite happiness, for God; it is certainly the deepest and most central instinct of the human soul (although, curiously, it hardly plays a role in current academic personality psychology). The purer the soul, the more this instinct is active. But according to St. Catherine, it is definitively released at this short, solemn, and determining moment when the bodiless soul stands before God,[6] Who has forgiven it its guilt and

> tugs at it with a glance, draws it and binds it to Himself with a fiery love that by itself could annihilate the immortal soul. In so acting, God so transforms the soul in Him that it knows nothing other than God; and he continues to draw it up into His fiery love until He restores it to that pure state from which it first issued. As it is being drawn upwards, the soul feels itself melting in the fire of that love of its sweet God."

Catherine of Genoa. Portrait painting in the Pammatone Hospital in Genoa.

In consequence, the soul is, on the one hand, "immersed in charity, incapable of deviating from it, [and] can only will or desire pure love. There is no joy save that in paradise to be compared to the joy of the souls in Purgatory. This joy increases day by day because of the way the love of God corresponds to that of the soul, since the impediment of that love is worn away daily." This is the joy of loving God and being loved by God. On the other hand, this same love is inhibited by the remaining "rust of sin" that impedes the soul to immediately attain its Bliss. Inhibited "fiery love" is the same as ardent longing, yearning, and utter thirstiness, and that means severe suffering. Here we come to St. Catherine's explanation of the tormenting flames of Purgatory:

> The greatest suffering of the souls in purgatory, it seems to me, is the awareness that something in them displeases God, that they have deliberately gone against His great goodness. . . . I can also see . . . that the divine essence is so pure and light-filled—much

more than we can imagine—that the soul that has but the slightest
imperfection would rather throw itself into a thousand hells than
appear thus before the divine presence." Hence "the soul . . . aware
that the impediment it faces cannot be removed in any other way,
hurls itself into purgatory. . . . That is why the soul seeks to cast off
any and all impediments so that it can be lifted up to God.

The purifying force of God's love is the essence of Purgatory. "In
considering how an impediment blocks our way to God, and for
what just reasons . . . [it] is impeded, the soul feels within it a fire like
that of hell, save that it has no sense of guilt."

✳   ✳   ✳

It is not difficult to see that this view is compatible with the traditional notion of the "pain of loss" (of God) as the main cause of the
souls' suffering, as the souls themselves made clear to St. Faustina on
her visit to Purgatory.

The paradox of Purgatory is this: in comparison with God's love,
"the suffering of purgatory is a small matter," and yet, "this harmony
with God's will also brings about a very great suffering. Its compre-
hension is beyond all words or thoughts." And again, "The overwhelming love of God gives [the soul] a joy beyond words. Yet this
joy does not do away with one bit of pain in the sufferings of the
souls in purgatory."

It is this unimaginable pain caused by the fire of love and longing that is communicated by all souls from Purgatory and tangibly
demonstrated in the burn marks in the *Museo del Purgatorio*. "A fire
like that of hell": in the opinion of St. Thomas, the proper fires of
Purgatory and Hell are one and the same.[7] Originally, the Jewish
Gehinnom also referred to the fire of Hell and Purgatory without distinction, a tradition that is still alive in the modern Orthodox Jewish
religion, along with the awareness that "all the suffering of Job would
not compare to an instant in gehinnom."[8] (This latter idea is also
taught by St. Augustine, St. Thomas, and St. Bernard.[9])

With respect to the torment of burning, many souls from Purgatory
indeed manifest themselves in flames; however, not all of them do. But
it is significant that those who show themselves not visibly ablaze

may still give proof of their burning in leaving some visible token of their presence. For example, a soul who appeared to the great helper of the poor souls, Mother Anna Maria Lindmayr (1657–1726), the "Saint of Munich," blew an ice-cold breath into her face, yet upon touching the sister's foot with a finger, it left a deep burn.[10]

The doctrine of St. Catherine puts our perception of the frightening, to some people even macabre pieces exhibited in the *Museo del Purgatorio*, in a more balanced perspective. Although the sufferings that left such concrete demonstrations of the souls' pain cannot be minimized, still they do not tell us the full tale of Purgatory. St. Catherine elucidates that their sufferings "are endurable because of two considerations. The first is their willingness to suffer, the certainty that God has been most merciful to them in the light of what they deserved . . . [they] accept the ordinance of God and would not think of doing otherwise. The other consideration that sustains those souls is a certain joy that is never wanting and that, indeed, increases as they come closer to God."

Her insight is echoed by St. Francis de Sales. He often reminded his priests that they should not only draw the attention of the faithful to the pain and punishment of the souls in Purgatory but also to "their perfect love of God" and to their joy of being in the state of grace and of being sure of their arrival at the blissful vision of God.[11]

※ ※ ※

Nonetheless, however mitigating these positive and encouraging considerations may be, they do not prevent a close look at the grim reality of Purgatory, as revealed by the apparitions of souls and their visible imprints, from causing the emotional reaction of shivering. We may suppose, however, that apart from stirring our compassion, this normal human reaction is also calculated to arouse a wholesome fear of sin. St. Catherine herself says that she "would want to frighten people, to cry out to each and everyone: 'O wretches who let yourselves be blinded in this world and make no provision for this one most important need [your preparation for the next world]! . . . His justice will not be wanting." In this connection, the observation of St. Teresa of Avila, the saint who often conversed with departed souls, is pertinent, namely, that "among all souls I have seen, there are only three who totally escaped purgatory."[12]

The speculation of Sister Lucia on the manner in which the soul is purified in Purgatory, which was prompted by the communication of Our Lady that a young girl from her village had to stay in Purgatory until the end of the world, seems to synchronize with the explanation of St. Catherine. Sister Lucia wrote, "What purifies is . . . the fire of divine love, which is conferred by God on the souls in proportion as every soul corresponds."[13] Thus both identify the love of God as the purifying agent. The soul's openness to God—that is, its love of God, the extent to which the will is directed to God at the moment of death (plus the quantity of "rust," the amount of debt, of punishment that is not atoned for)—determines how much purifying fire, how much love from God, it is able to absorb.

This is in line with the teaching of St. Francis de Sales on the operation of God's love in man in general, in this world or in the next:

> In the same measure in which our heart dilates itself, or rather in the measure in which it permits itself to be enlarged and dilated, keeping itself empty by the simple fact of not refusing consent to the divine mercy, this ever pours forth and ceaselessly spreads its sacred inspirations, which ever increase and make us increase more and more in heavenly love; but when there is no more room, that is, when we no longer give consent, it stops. How comes it that we are not so advanced in the love of God as St. Augustine, St. Francis, etc.? Theotimus [the name he gives his listener or reader], it is because God has not given us the grace. But why has he not given us the grace? Because we did not correspond to his inspirations as we should have done.[14]

CHAPTER 8

THE EXHIBITS OF
THE MUSEUM OF PURGATORY

*T*he modest "museum" in a room of the sacristy of the church of the Sacred Heart of Suffrage consists of ten specimens or relics, exhibited behind glass. Its story began in 1893, when Father Victor Jouët (1839–1912) built in the place of the present church a chapel for the so-called Arch-confraternity of the Sacred Heart of Jesus for Aid to the Holy Souls, which he had founded.[1]

In November 1897, the altar in the chapel caught fire. Many people who were present thought they discerned through the flames, on the left side of the altar, the face of an anguished person. Whether it was truly an apparition of a soul from Purgatory, one can still see the distorted features of this face on the wall, which was conserved when the chapel was demolished and the present church completed in 1917. At present, it is concealed behind a triptych of Our Lady with the angels, as the museum's first "exhibit." Shown below as **Exhibits 1a–1c**.

Father Jouët began to collect testimonies, documents, and objects that could help to incite devotion to the poor souls. The exhibition he made of them was originally larger than the present

Father Victor Jouët, founder of the Museo del Purgatorio.

one, because one of his successors later removed those items whose documentation could be open to some criticism. The remaining pieces span more than two centuries; the oldest belongs to an apparition from 1696, the most recent from 1919. (More recent apparitions of souls from Purgatory have also been well documented, as we shall discuss later. But it does not seem that any systematic attempt has been made to collect evidence of burn marks since the work of Father Jouët—in part due to the waning belief in Purgatory, one might wonder.) Due to the difficulties of traveling and communication at the time the pieces were gathered, they all come from western European countries: Germany, Belgium, France, Austria, and Italy. (Yet they are not the only ones in existence, as we shall see in later chapters.) Two popes have supported and patronized the work of the archconfraternity founded by Father Jouët, as well as the building of the church of the Sacred Heart of Suffrage: Pope Pius X and Pope Benedict XV.

✴ ✴ ✴

Let us now inspect the visible signals from Purgatory of the *Museo del Purgatorio*.

These physical objects with evident burn marks are carefully examined, and humanly speaking it must be excluded that they are fakes: first, because they are attested to by honest and reliable witnesses and authenticated by various diocesan authorities after critical examination, and second, due to the nature of the evidence itself. It is virtually impossible in most cases artificially to produce burn traces or marks such as those we encounter here in prayer books or tissues,

Exhibit 1a: The face that was left on the wall of the chapel after the fire.

Exhibit 1b: Triptych covering the preserved wall of the chapel with the face.

Exhibit 1c: Here, the left part of the triptych (with the face behind it) has been removed.

and in some cases it seems even entirely impossible, as with objects like the prayer book of Hall.[2]

Certainly, we would like to have more information about questions relating to many apparitions of the past and about the relics connected with them, and it is to be hoped that these relics will some day be examined with the methods of modern forensic technology. Yet the silent assumption that many moderns make—that all people in former ages were credulous and uncritical—is fully groundless. There are countless and extensive reports and affidavits to give the lie to it. In fact, many conscientious priests and other investigators saw it as their dire duty to uncover the truth and expose frauds or superstition, and they undertook their investigations with a sound dose of skepticism. Similarly, most seers of poor souls initially doubted their senses, too; this is a normal, healthy reaction. The point is that one has to be not only critical of alleged supernatural phenomena but also critical of the tendency to reject on *a priori* grounds the undeniable evidence of a reality that cannot be grasped in terms of the concrete, material reality surrounding us.

Exhibit 2: Three fingers on the prayer book of Maria Zaganti

Exhibit 2: A prayer book with three burned-in fingerprints of the ghost of Palmira Rastelli.

The book belonged to Maria Zaganti of the parish of St. Andrew in Poggio Berni (Rimini, Italy). Palmira was the sister of the parish priest and had died on December 28, 1870. She appeared to her friend Maria Zaganti, on March 5, 1871, and asked her for holy Masses to be offered by her brother, Don Sante Rastelli. At that time, she was a little over two months in Purgatory.[3]

Exhibit 3: Burn marks of five fingers on the nightcap of Louis Le Sénèchal, left by the ghost of his wife Louise.

Louise Sénèchal died on May 7, 1873, and about two years later appeared to her husband at their house in Ducey, France, requesting

Exhibit 3: Burns of the thumb and fingertips (slightly visible) on the nightcap of Mr. Le Sénèchal, with seals of parish and diocese.

Exhibit 4: Photography of hand imprint on the apron of Sister Herendorps and two hands of the apparition on a strip of linen.

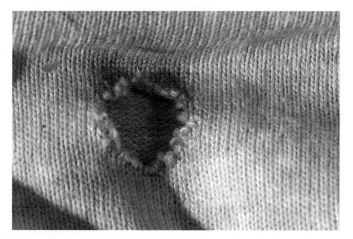

Exhibit 3: Close-up of burn hole of the thumb in the night cap.

that Masses be said for her. The document accompanying the night-cap mentions that the burn mark was intended by Louise as proof for her husband to convince their daughter, in order to substantiate Louise's request for the Masses.

Exhibit 4: Photocopy of burn marks left by a Benedictine choir sister named Clara Schoelers.

The original objects are kept in the Benedictine monastery of Vinnenberg (near Warendorf, Germany). Schoelers appeared there to Maria Herendorps, a lay sister of the monastery, on October 13, 1696. Her hands left burn marks on Herendorps's apron and also on a piece of linen. She had died of the plague in 1637, and thus had been in Purgatory for 59 years.

Exhibit 5: Photocopy of a burned-in handprint left on the sleeve of Joseph Leleux by the ghost of his mother.

For 11 consecutive nights, in his house at Wodecq in Belgium, Leleux had heard noises that terribly frightened him and made him almost sick.[4] Then on the night of June 21, 1789, his mother appeared and reminded him that he was under obligation, according to the terms of the legacy of his father, to have celebrated holy Masses. She reproached him for his dissolute way of life and begged him to

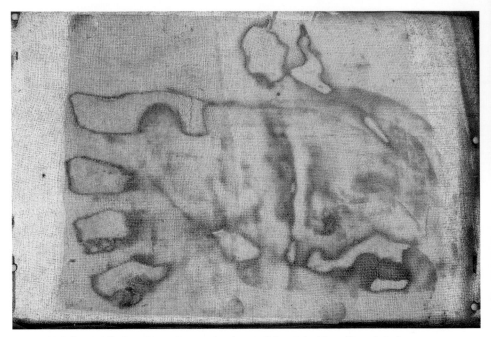

Exhibit 5: The hand imprint on the sleeve of the nightshirt of Joseph Leleux.

change his behavior[5] and to work for the Church. Then she laid her
hand on the sleeve of his nightshirt.

Mrs. Leleux had been dead for 27 years when she appeared.

Joseph Leleux converted and founded a congregation of pious lay
people. He died in the odor of sanctity on April 19, 1825.

Exhibit 6: A fiery imprint of a forefinger on the pillow of Sister Margherita of the Sacred Heart of the monastery of St. Clare of the Child Jesus in Bastia, Italy.

This mark was left on the night of June 5, 1894, when the deceased
Sister Maria of St. Louis de Gonzaga appeared to Sister Margaret.
According to the account of the event, which is preserved in the monastery, the deceased, who had been a pious nun, appeared dressed as
a Poor Clare sister, surrounded by shadows but recognizable. To the
surprise of Sister Margaret, she explained that she was in Purgatory
to expiate for her bouts of impatience, her not accepting God's will.

The deceased had suffered for about two years from tuberculosis, severe fever, coughing, and asthma and had given in to a fit of discouragement, desiring to die at once rather than suffer any longer. However, as she was a very fervent soul, upon the exhortation of her Mother Superior, she had resigned herself to God's will. A few days later, she had died a holy death that very morning of June 5.

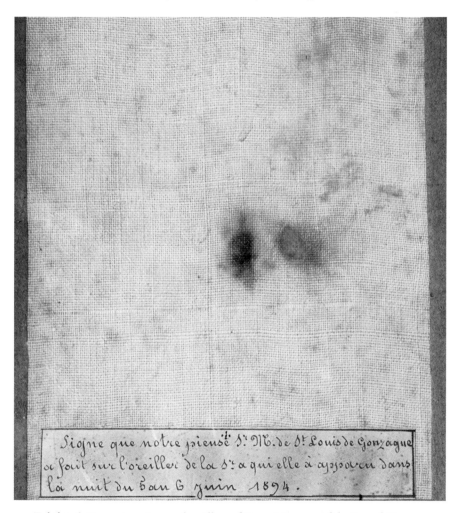

Exhibit 6: Finger imprint on the pillow of Sister Margaret of the Sacred Heart. Underneath in French: "Sign which our pious Sister M. de St. Louis de Gonzaga made on the pillow of the Sister to whom she appeared in the night of 5 to 6 June, 1894."

She asked for prayers of suffrage, put her finger on the pillow, and promised to return. Indeed, she reappeared to the same nun, on June 20 and 25, to thank her and give spiritual advice to the community, before she went to Heaven.

When souls of persons who had been good or pious during their earthly life appear to ask for help, our understandable reaction is one of surprise. Such apparitions, however, demonstrate the teaching of St. Catherine of Genoa that even the smallest imperfections or "stains" left by sins must be burned away and that the judgment of the living is often too light-hearted and superficial. These apparitions caution against the neglect of prayer for those who are too rashly thought to be "already in heaven."

Otherwise, it may seem that the piety and fervor of Sister Maria were rewarded in that she was permitted to ask for suffrages the very night of her death (and not after a long time, as in other cases) and to give a clinching signal that aroused the effective compassion of her community.

Exhibits 7a–d: Four burn marks left by the ghost of one Father Panzini, a former abbot from Mantua, Italy.[6]

Father Panzini appeared on November 1, 1731, the eve of All Souls' Day, to the venerable Mother Isabella Fornari, abbess of the Poor Clares of the monastery of St. Francis in Todi. He left one mark from his left hand, plus a Sign of the Cross burned deeply into the wood of Mother Isabella's worktable; one of the same left hand on a sheet of paper; and finally, on Mother Isabella's tunic, the imprint of a burn that passed right through and also burned the sleeve of her chemise. The last one is stained with blood.

It is plausible that this soul came to Mother Isabella because the intercession of holy souls has the most effect (Mother Isabella was a "venerable"). Father Isidoro Gazala of the Blessed Crucifix, confessor of the abbess, wrote a report of the event and ordered the abbess to cut off from her tunic and chemise the parts bearing the marks and hand all objects over to him to preserve them.

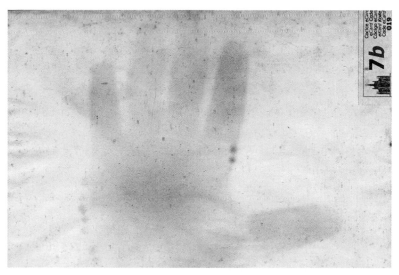

Exhibit 7a: Left hand of the apparition to Mother Fornari on sheet of paper.

Exhibit 7b: Same left hand and cross on wooden table of Mother Fornari.

Exhibit 7c: Right hand on the sleeve of the tunic of Mother Fornari (fragment).

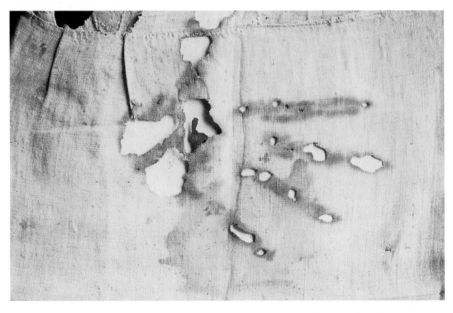

Exhibit 7d: Same right hand on the (cutoff) sleeve of the chemise of Mother Fornari (with some blood stains; the hand had been scorched through the tunic).

Exhibit 8: Burned-in hand on a copy of *The Imitation of Christ* belonging to Marguérite Demmerlé of the parish of Ellenghen (diocese of Metz, now France).

This burn mark was left by her mother-in-law when she appeared to Marguérite in 1815, 30 years after her death. The deceased appeared dressed as a pilgrim in the traditional costume of her country; she was coming down the stairs of the barn, sighing and staring sadly at her daughter-in-law, as if she wanted to beg for something.

In a subsequent apparition, following the advice of the parish priest, Marguérite dared to address her and got this response: "I am your mother-in-law who died at childbirth, thirty years ago. Go on

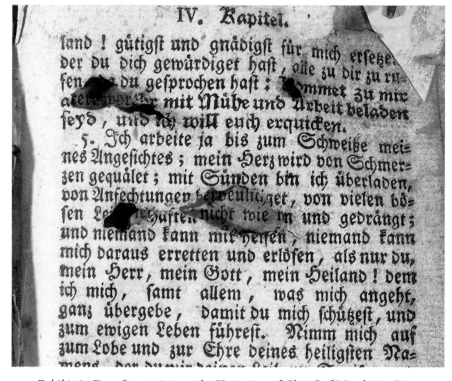

Exhibit 8: Fiery fingerprints on the "Imitation of Christ" of Marghérite Demmerlé, on the text in book 4: "Yet whatever fails me, good Jesus . . . may You supply it most leniently and mercifully. . . . Truly I labor in the sweat of my face, my heart is tormented by grief, I am laden with sins, . . . and no one can liberate and save me, but You, my Savior."

pilgrimage to the sanctuary of Our Lady of Marienthal and have two Masses said for me there."

After the pilgrimage, the mother-in-law showed herself to Marguérite to announce her liberation from Purgatory. When her daughter-in-law, again on the advice of the parish priest, asked her for a signal, she put her hand on the book and left the burn mark. Afterward, she appeared no more.

The literature on Purgatory has more examples of poor souls who request a holy Mass in a Marian sanctuary, no doubt for its special value of expiation due to her special intervention.

Exhibit 9: Burn marks left by the ghost of Joseph Schitz on the prayer book of his brother Georg.

On December 21, 1838, Joseph appeared to his brother at his home in Sarralbe (Lorraine, at the time not a part of France). He touched the prayer book and asked for prayers of suffrage to make satisfaction for his lack of piety during his life on earth.

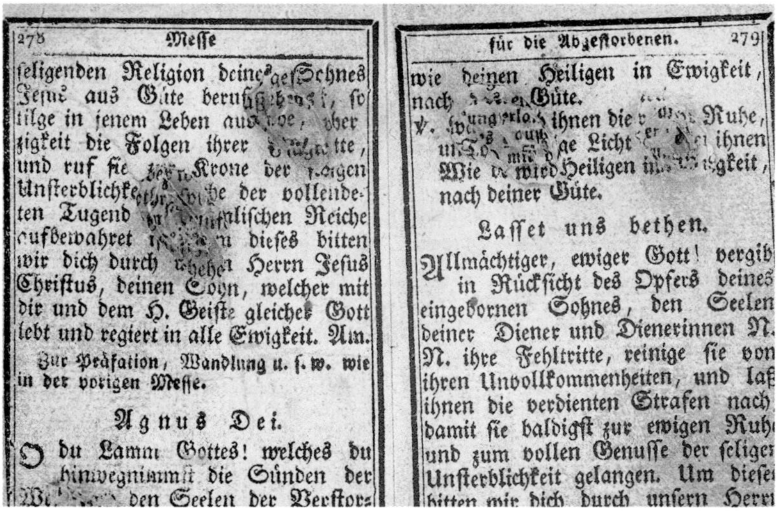

Exhibit 9: Fingertips of right hand on prayer book of Georg Schitz, placed on the prayers of the Requiem Mass: "Grant the souls of the departed eternal rest . . ." This suggests that the deceased urged his brother to have a Requiem Mass said for him and say the prayers for the dead.

It is stupendous that the fiery fingerprints on the prayer book do not appear to be placed at random but deliberately on determinate pages, as if the deceased wanted to draw the attention to the prayers printed there. The relic shows fingerprints on a prayer containing the words "thus discharge in that life hereafter by mercy the consequences of their trespasses, and call them to the crown of the . . . immortality . . . of the accomplished virtue in the heavenly kingdom . . ." and "(grant) the

FRONT

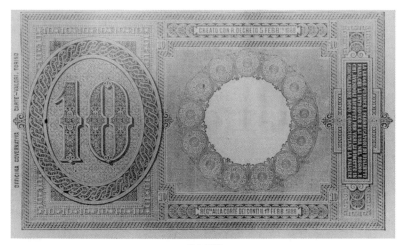

BACK

Exhibit 10: Photocopy of a ten lire note (two sides).

souls of the defunct the eternal rest . . . " and "(grant) them the eternal rest, and the (eternal) Light may enlighten them."[7] All these passages are fragments of the prayers of the Requiem Mass for the dead: a silent but eloquent message!

Exhibit 10: Photocopy of an Italian banknote of ten lire, left by a deceased Italian priest who asked for holy Masses.

Thirty such notes were left at the monastery of St. Leonardo, in Montefalco, Italy, between August 18 and November 9, 1919, by the ghost of a priest who requested that the money pay for holy Masses. The original of this note has been returned to the monastery of St. Leonardo where it is still preserved.

❋ ❋ ❋

It is remarkable that several of these specimens either come from apparitions of religious or priests or were directed to religious. This might be explained in part by the fact that such specimens are likely to be better preserved by religious communities. But it is quite possible too that, on the one hand, the suffering souls of religious are more frequently allowed by God to ask for assistance; and on the other hand, that the piety of the living—be they religious, priests, or lay people—is often a requirement that must be met before poor souls are permitted to come and ask for help.

❋ ❋ ❋

One will never find a collection comparable to that in the Little Museum outside the Catholic Church. Taken together, the exhibits are convincing testimony of the Catholic doctrine of Purgatory, for the humble Christian believer as well as for the sincerely investigative seeker of truth about the hereafter. Much more than fascinating souvenirs of merely "private revelations," these fiery imprints of fingers and hands have been allowed or ordered by the Almighty so that their images, in turn, will be indelibly imprinted on our mind and on our memory, as eloquent visual lessons. That is why the great Pope Pius X was very interested and content when, in August 1905, the objects of the collection that had been acquired at the time were shown to him in one of the rooms of the Vatican.

It is clear which lessons are meant: principally, that of the duty of the living to help the suffering souls. In a double sense, these objects express an ardent appeal to wake up from our forgetfulness and lethargy with respect to the dead and to start praying for them, offering up holy Masses for them. That appeal is very much needed today. Purgatory must be taught again by priests in the church, by parents to their children, by friends to their friends. We help the hungry and needy in this world but neglect those in the next who are even hungrier and needier.

Pope John Paul II insisted that the "solidarity" with the poor souls "should be re-proposed today." An indispensable part of such "re-proposal," however, is lifting the prevailing ignorance about Purgatory. To this end, the collection in the museum is an effective instruction tool. And when, after some time, our zeal to come to the aid of the suffering souls will be flagging, looking again at the pictures of these exhibits and rereading the accompanying stories will help to reinvigorate it.

The other important lesson, for us, is the inconceivable seriousness of sin and evil and the necessity to strive after holiness in our daily life. Within a couple of years or decades, we will find ourselves in the same situation as the countless poor dead at this moment. Who will help us then? Many appearing souls from Purgatory (as well as great saints) have warned us living to apply to ourselves the lesson about the necessity of hard atonement. Fear of Purgatory is perhaps not the highest, certainly not the exclusive, motive to strive after holiness, but it is a very human incentive that must not be despised. Some forms of fear are salutary; they can help discerning realities we otherwise would hardly be open to.

Then there are the greatly consoling lessons. In fact, Purgatory is immersed in the mercy of the good God. It ends up in unimaginable happiness: Heaven. God alleviates and abbreviates the expiating suffering in Purgatory, among other things, by stimulating the living to come to their aid and, of course, in a mysterious way, by enkindling an ardent love of Him in the soul that is about to enter Purgatory, so that it seems that at least many souls there are not deprived of great joys.

In concord with St. Catherine of Genoa, Padre Pio has spoken of the "atrocious pains" of the soul that is purified, whether on this earth or in Purgatory, so as to be able to be united with God; but on the other hand, he balanced this daunting aspect of the purification process: "Purgatory is sweet when one suffers for the love of God."[8] In spite of Purgatory's shocking gravity, meditation on it should not make us depressed, but rather hopeful, because this reality is embedded in love, purity, supernatural serenity, and beauty. Father Jouët, the founder of the museum, summed up the above lessons when he referred to it as this "Christian museum which has been formed so providentially, and of which the teachings on Purgatory are at the same time so grave and so consoling."[9]

CHAPTER 9

THE BURNED-IN
HAND OF CZESTOCHOWA

*A*fter the human face, the hand is the member of the body that most represents and expresses the individuality of a person. It is conspicuous that souls from Purgatory do not leave imprints or images of the face they had during life—with the rare exception, probably, of that intriguing face on the wall during and after the fire in the chapel devoted to the holy souls in November 1897. If this is really an image of a soul from Purgatory, which it seems to be, there must have been a reason for this remarkable exception to the rule. Was it a perhaps a special privilege to confirm and encourage the specific work of charity performed and promoted in this sacred place, to invite the faithful to exercise the devotion to the Sacred Heart of Suffrage, as if to say that, here, the poor souls are spiritually very near the faithful who pray for them?

In order to prove that they have really been "there and then" and that their requests were authentically theirs, as we saw in the examples from the previous chapter, souls from Purgatory typically stamp their hand or fingers in some tissue, book, or wooden object, as in former days when important documents were authenticated by stamping the author's wax seal on it. With this hand, the person did his work; his handshake brought him in closer contact with us; his hand may have lovingly caressed or struck in anger, communicated emotions, or been folded in prayer. When it is impressed by a soul from Purgatory, it is in fact also a supplicating hand.[1] Some hands from Purgatory are particularly impressive as their anatomy distinctly shows personal characteristics. And they are placed so thoughtfully, almost artistically, that they silently but eloquently express a profound mystery.

The "Black Madonna." The miraculous icon of Our Lady, Queen of Poland, in the chapel of Our Lady at Jasna Góra, Czestochowa.

✳   ✳   ✳

One of the most beautiful examples of a hand mark left by a holy soul is that of a defunct priest, whose hand burned into a *corporale*, a fine linen cloth used in the Mass to cover the chalice. This precious item is preserved in the monastery of the Paulinian Order, which is part of the national Polish sanctuary of Czestochowa, located on a hill within the city that bears the name of Jasna Góra, the "bright hill." The basilica on Jasna Góra attracts a constant stream of pilgrims who come to see and venerate the famous icon of the "Black Madonna," incontestably one of the world's most beautiful and moving images of the Blessed Virgin. The Paulinian Fathers of the convent have the task to minister to the church.

The *corporale* with the burned-in hand is not publicly exhibited.[2] Rather, it is carefully packed in a tin box with a glass lid, the kind of boxes in the late 19th century to preserve photographs.[3] This suggests that the event that caused the imprint of the fiery right hand is to be dated not much after 1880. Unfortunately, if there was ever an official document describing the paranormal occurrences surrounding the burn mark, it has been lost for quite some time.[4] The oldest testimony we can find is a report of probably 1890 by one Father Reichel, the parish priest of Hundsfeld, near Wroclaw (then Breslau). These are his words:[5]

> I was with two confreres on pilgrimage in Czestochowa. When a friar of the monastery, who had the supervision of the sacristy, showed us the noteworthy things, he led us also into an adjoining vault and showed us there among other things, out of special kindness, remarking that this was done only exceptionally, a square tin box with lid; he lifted this, and we saw lying in it a *corporale* on which a human hand that must have been red-hot had been impressed. The upper layers of the linen were totally burned through, the lower were browned, increasingly more lightly; in the deeper parts between the individual joints the folds of the linen were conserved [visible], there where the muscles are more articulate [thicker], the combustion was quite visibly stronger, decreasing gradually to the sides. The following had occurred:

Two clerics of the monastery (of the Paulinian Order) had promised one another many years ago that the one who would die first would give the other one a sign from the beyond. Now one of them was dead already for a long time[6] and never had given a sign. This was what the other one was thinking about, when one day he just had finished holy Mass and, as usual, was folding together the *corporale* before him, in nine folds. Then the evil doubt went through his head that perhaps there would be no survival after death at all. At that moment, a hand appears, lays itself on the corporale, and immediately disappears again.[7] How much it was ablaze through and through, however, is shown clearly enough by the combustion of the nine-times folded up linen, exactly in the form of the hand.

The corporale with the burned-in hand in a little case from the end of the 19th century.

Upper layer of the folded corporale. It is clear that it had not been folded up completely at the moment the hand imprint was made. Where the fingers come in direct contact with the tissue, it has been scorched through and through.

The corporale is being unfolded.

This interesting account still leaves open several questions, apart from the problem of the dating of this mystical event. Could the priest have recognized the hand of his dead confrere? Was it only the hand that appeared, or was more of the dead priest visible? If so, did he speak? Assuming that he was in Purgatory, what suffrage was offered him, and did he appear again (perhaps to announce his deliverance)? How long was the deceased in Purgatory?

These gaps in our information aside, the story as it was told by the Paulinian friar to Father Reichel and his companions contains a few notable points. Apparently, the agreement of the two priests was honored by Heaven, as in the case of a similar agreement Don Bosco had made with his friend Luigi Comollo—very imprudently, as he confessed later on.[8] The surviving Paulinian Father got his answer, not in the way he may have anticipated, but in the way ordained by God. It can certainly be viewed as a gracious gesture on the part of his deceased friend to place his hand so delicately on the already more than halfway folded up *corporale* that only the upper layers were burned and the underlying altar cloth remained fully undamaged, and whereby he mercifully and in one stroke put an end to

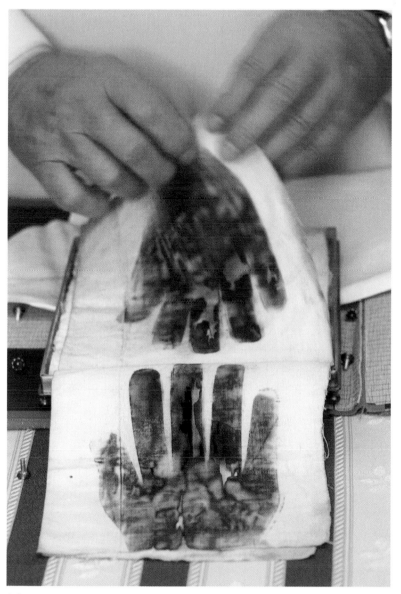

The two upper layers. Visible is the difference in intensity of the scorching imprint of the hand on the two layers.

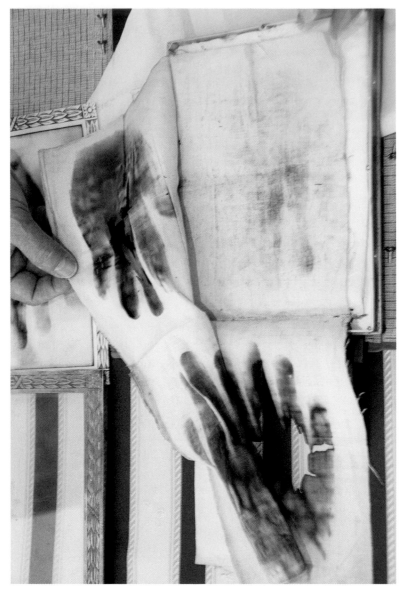

The unfolded corporale. The upper layers are burned through; below them the hand imprint gets a lighter color and it is just light brown on the undermost layer (the altar cloth under the corporale was wholly undamaged).

Father Melchior Królik, the curator of the library and the archive of the monastery of Jasna Góra, and author Dr. Gerard van den Aardweg putting the corporale back in the case.

his friend's religious doubts. But at the same time, the sudden and frightening way the deceased fulfilled his promise, completely unexpected, has a serious lesson: eternity is a tremendous mystery, nothing to play with out of immature curiosity. The reaction from the other side of the grave of his dear friend Luigi Comollo had inculcated the same lesson in the mind of the young Don Bosco.[9]

CHAPTER 10

OTHER EXAMPLES OF BURN MARKS

*T*he Museum of Purgatory's collection is extensive but far from exhaustive. There are descriptions of objects with burned-in hand marks in various Catholic regions.[1] Thus the monastery of the Franciscan nuns of St. Ann at Foligno (Italy) possessed the hand imprint of the deceased Sister Teresia Margarita Gesta on the door of the linen room, "better and more clear than if made with a glowing iron hand." The imprint dates to November 3, 1859, and already on the 23rd of that month an official examination was being conducted. It turned out that the hand of the deceased nun fitted exactly the burn mark on the door.[2]

The following are some other examples:

> Five burn marks of a hand were left by the deceased Johann Klements during his many apparitions between 1641 and 1642 in Pressburg/Poszony (today Bratislava, Slovakia). The remarkable case was examined and published in 1643 by the bishop, and included the affidavits of thirty-two persons who had had been witness to some of the apparitions.[3] Significantly, Johann Klements

was missing the upper phalanx of his right forefinger, and this is
also missing in the hand marks.

The parish archive of Pflochsbach on the Main (Germany) preserved the burned-in hand mark in a handkerchief left during an
apparition around 1750, as well as a series of accompanying documents on the apparition.[4]

The Augustinian monastery in Fuchsmühl (Germany) preserved
a piece of cloth with the burn mark of a hand made during a
well-documented apparition on April 4, 1736.[5] The night before,
a woman who had died 34 years prior appeared to her daughter-
in-law and asked for holy Masses of suffrage. At the second apparition, the seer, in the company of her husband and two other
men, asked the ghost for proof of her real presence, whereupon
the departed soul requested a piece of cloth and struck with a hard
and loud blow an imprint of her hand into it. The three men (aged
56, 46, and 44 years) testified under oath that although they had
not seen the apparition, they had heard it, and that they had also
heard the loud blow.

The burned-in thumb in a prayer book at Hall in Tirol (Austria) is
rather well known.[6] It was produced in 1669 by Vicar Christoph
Wallbach, who had died on May 5, 1605, at one of his apparitions to the housekeeper of one of his successors. The deceased
left this impressive sign to make it clear how terrible a fire it was
he was in, because on earth he had read holy Masses out of ava-
rice, for the money he could get; also, he wanted to prove that his
appearance was no illusion. He was already in Purgatory for 65
years, and, in a remarkable detail, he revealed that he would have
to suffer for another 50 years if he were not released by suffrages
during the half-year granted him to ask for help. In fact, this ghost
had manifested itself already for a longer period through "spook"
phenomena: scratching, fist blows on the wall, rapping, noises as
if someone were walking through the presbytery, moaning. One
time the housekeeper saw the ghost in the church, dressed as a
priest of former days. Although he had been noticed by her more
often, he had never spoken until she mustered up her courage and

asked him what he wanted. Various persons, among them the parish priest, witnessed the manifestations and heard the moaning.

The thumb burn in the prayer book of Hall went right through a heavy cover of wood and pigskin and then through 40 pages and, decreasing in intensity, through 30 more pages. It must have been produced during one short, intense moment, for there are no traces of burning beside the burned-in hole.[7] A blacksmith experimented with a glowing iron thumb but could not nearly reproduce the phenomenon himself; instead, the whole paper burned. (Likewise, artificially burned-in hands do not show the typical features of burn marks created by the departed.[8])

In Merl, a village near Echternach (Luxembourg), a deceased father appeared to his daughter in 1865, requesting of her several prayer-marches to the nearby sanctuary of St. Gangolf. He left a burn mark of his hand in a prayer book and in a handkerchief. Several persons witnessed how the young woman, who apparently saw her father's ghost in the church of Merl (although they did not see it), took her handkerchief, whereupon it was suddenly grasped and thrown away as if by an invisible hand. When she picked it up from the floor, it was marked by the burn.[9]

On April 4, 1922, a woman who attended a Mass celebrated for a departed priest in a church in the Saarland (Germany) saw two times (during the entrance prayer and when the epistle was read) an apparition of a priest surrounded by flames, leafing through the pages of an altar missal. The apparition had given her to understand that he suffered because of a photograph of him, which was in the possession of a certain lady whose name and address the apparition revealed. The seer did not know the priest and had never been in the place where the lady lived; nor did she know that the intention of this holy Mass was precisely for this priest, who had passed away just a week before. When she told the celebrating priest what she had seen, he inspected the altar missal and discovered that some pages bore the inexplicable burning marks of the thumb and forefinger of a right hand (the fingers that had leafed through the book) and, moreover, that the marks were placed on specific supplicating prayers for the deceased, such as "We pray

Thee, o Lord, have mercy on the soul of your servant, N., for whom we offer up this Sacrifice of praise, we humbly supplicate Thy Majesty: let him come to eternal rest through this Sacrifice of reconciliation."[10]

The priest verified the affirmation about the photograph, which was indeed in the possession of the lady in question; upon seeing it, the seer recognized the deceased priest.[11]

As in the case of the apparition of Joseph Schitz in 1838 (the ninth item of the collection in the Museo del Purgatorio), the deceased likely placed his fingers on the prayers he wanted to highlight. And there are more such examples.[12]

CHAPTER 11

HOW THE POOR SOULS
APPEAR, AND TO WHOM

*I*mmaterial spirits take on material forms to make themselves visible, and these forms express essential features of their spiritual and moral state of being. Demons appear as repulsive creatures; if they disguise themselves as human persons, there is usually some abhorrent quality of shape or manners that puts the seer on his guard. An angel may appear "as a light whiter than snow in the form of a young man, quite transparent and brilliant as crystal," as the Angel of Portugal in the story of Fatima,[1] thus expressing his heavenly origin.

The ghostly forms of souls from Purgatory show, on the one hand, recognizable characteristics of the face and body that they animated during earthly life—and with which they will be united on the day of general judgment. On the other hand, the appearance of the ghost sometimes symbolizes its state of suffering and/or its individual moral imperfections: the "rust of sin" not yet cleaned off, the imperfect habits and tendencies that the person carried with him across the threshold into the afterlife.

These apparitions clearly prove that it is the individual *person* and not some depersonalized, anonymous "soul matter" that survives bodily death. The reports of so many seers over the centuries are doubtless reports of *direct contacts* with a supernatural reality and with real persons. If there is much symbolic in the way they appear, these symbols seem to be the most appropriate method to bring the living as near to the supernatural reality of Purgatory as they can possibly come.

In some mysterious way, the deceased *is* present, there and then, in the place and in the moment he appears. At the onset of an apparition, the seer and bystanders often observe physical phenomena such as atmospheric changes, a gust of cold wind, crackling sounds, a strange and sudden silence; the spirit develops its figure and form out of a hazy cloud or mist, or starts as a passing shadow. It is not unusual for animals to perceive something physical, too: dogs may become scared, and cattle or chickens become restless. The perception of a spirit cannot be reduced to a merely mental event, something internal in the seer; it is a manifestation outside of him. He can see the door opening or a strange light that makes the objects in the dark room visible; objects (such as a light-switch on the wall) cannot be perceived anymore during the time the phantom stands before it, but as soon as it is gone, the object is normally visible again.[2]

✳   ✳   ✳

There are roughly three variants of the visible forms or figures of appearing poor souls: either they come in the figures of the persons they were in life, with their typical clothes; amid flames; or again, as deformed humans with remarkable symbolic features that represent their sins and/or punishments—sometimes even as humanized animals or animalized humans. Ghosts from Purgatory are as a rule recognizable by their eyes and mouth, wrote the 20th-century seer Eugenie von der Leyen. "You never see such eyes in men . . . they demonstrate, or give to understand, misery. The mouth . . . this bitterness is found in no [living] human."[3]

The saintly Bavarian mystic, Sister Maria Anna Lindmayr (1657 1726), regularly saw the poor souls in a manner that characterized the spiritual or moral state of their souls. Their features symbolized their vices as well as the kind of punishment they suffered:

> I have always been given to understand that: how you sin, so you must do penance . . . [Some] appeared to me very hungry, emaciated, in an indescribable form. These implored me to help them by fasting severely on water and bread, to correct what was wanting in them during their lifetime by their eating and drinking well and abundantly. Others again made known by their behavior their quick-temperedness and impatience and they implored me to help them by acts of patience and meekness. Such souls . . . were shown to me, their mouth locked with a nail.[4]

Some souls do not show the fire they are in, at least not initially, but appear as they had been in life. A deceased friend of Maria Anna walked before her on the street when she went to church, early in the morning; this happened so naturally that the seer "did not give it a thought, otherwise I would have been frightened," and only when she was in the church did she realize what she had seen (by then the apparition had vanished).[5] In a subsequent apparition, although no trace of burning or flames had been visible when it had manifested itself as the woman on her way to church, this same soul nonetheless demonstrated that it was burning by touching the foot of the seer "with a glowing finger."[6]

The visible appearance of the soul of a woman who came to Eugenie von der Leyen changed in response to the question of the seer:

"Do you then suffer so much?"

"Look at me!" was the soul's reply. Then she was as if flooded with fire.[7]

✳   ✳   ✳

It is sometimes thought that the strange or fantastic—and of course, symbolic—forms sometimes adopted by souls from Purgatory, and the severity of the punishments in that abode, are merely products of the romantic imaginations of certain cultural periods, notably the

Middle Ages and the Baroque. That theory, however, becomes rather improbable if we look at various trustworthy reports of well-examined apparitions made to psychologically healthy, virtuous, and even saintly persons of those periods, and then compare them to reports from less "imaginative" ages. The Servant of God, Mother Maria Anna Lindmayr, a balanced personality in the age of the Baroque, displayed a quite natural, sober attitude when she wrote that she "could never have imagined that things were that harsh in purgatory; yes, no one would be able to grasp it. I was instructed, though, by this [poor] soul [a deceased friend who repeatedly appeared to her in 1690], and so I could afterwards believe what otherwise I would never have believed."[8] This kind of apparition does not differ much either from those of earlier times or from those of more rationalistic ages closer to our own century.[9]

Moreover, it has always been believed, from the Church Fathers on, and in the Jewish tradition as well, that the sufferings of Purgatory surpass all terrestrial sufferings, so that the sometimes terrible images seen by those with whom the poor souls enter into contact, although "symbolic," can hardly be qualified as exaggerations of the imagination.

✳   ✳   ✳

It cannot escape us that the seers of souls from Purgatory are often reported to be especially good and pious persons. That sounds logical, for God permits a soul to appear so that it can be released from Purgatory, or at least, that its suffering be mitigated, and the pious (or at least, compassionate) person is more likely to respond to its requests. (Of course, God may choose others for one reason or another.) These considerations may also explain why apparitions from Purgatory and burned-in hands are predominantly (exclusively?) found in Catholic regions, more precisely, when and where Catholicism is flourishing, especially the devotion to the holy souls.[10]

Many canonized saints have been great helpers of the suffering souls. To honor the saints who are known for promoting devotion to these souls, the facade of the church of the Sacred Heart of Suffrage in Rome is adorned with beautiful statues of St. Augustine, St. Dominic, St. Francis Xavier, St. Victor, St. Francis of Assisi, St. Nicolas of Tolentino, St. Margaret Mary Alacoque, St. Catherine of Genoa, St. Bernard of Clairvaux, St. Gregory the Great, and St. Odilon of Cluny. On its stained-glass windows are the images of many famous saintly helpers of the poor souls: St. Francesca Romana, St. Bridget, St. Ambrose, St. Bonaventure, St. Thomas Aquinas, St. Efraim, St. Peter Damian, St. Francis de Sales, again St. Catherine of Genoa, and others. As we shall see in later chapters, several recently canonized saints have also been zealous helpers of the "holy souls," including Padre Pio, Josemaría Escrivá, and Sister Faustina.

The poor souls themselves sometimes express a preference for visiting persons who are generous enough to respond to their supplications with often great sacrifices. "What then can I poor wretch give you for special help?" Mother Maria Anna Lindmayr asked a supplicating soul. "My child!" was the reply, "How is it with people on earth? Don't they like to be with their friends and benefactors? Therefore we, too, like to be with you."[11] To a similar question, Eugenie von der Leyen got similar answers (from various souls): "You have always prayed for me" . . . "You attract us" . . . "The purer you are, the more you can help us" . . . "We are without pain when we are near you."[12]

Thus many saints were regularly visited by poor souls. It is also true that certain other persons appear to have been specifically called to holiness by devoting their life in a heroic way to the alleviation or deliverance of the suffering souls.[13] Their charity helps the poor souls while at the same time purifying and sanctifying themselves. Are there more women than men among these unselfish and spiritually privileged people? It would seem so, if we go by the documented reports about persons who entertained such self-sacrificing, intensive relationships with the poor souls.[14] Should this correlation with the female sex be confirmed, it might be explained by the motherly, caring, and more compassionate nature of the woman.

CHAPTER 12

BLESSED STANISLAUS PAPCZYNSKI:
AN EXTRAORDINARY FRIEND
TO THE SUFFERING SOULS

*F*ather Stanislaus Papczynski (1630–1701), the founder of the Congregation of the Immaculate Conception, the so-called Marian Fathers, is hardly known outside Poland and even less as a promoter of the charity for the souls in Purgatory. Yet he ranks among the foremost "apostle[s] of intercessory prayer for the dead," as Pope Benedict XVI honored him on occasion of his beatification in 2006.

In beatifying him, the church has implicitly recognized his specific way of helping the suffering souls, namely, commending them to the Blessed Virgin in her quality as the Immaculate Conception. That might have seemed rather audacious and original in his time, 200 years before the proclamation of the dogma of the Immaculate Conception, but Father Papczynski did not invent the idea himself. This combination of devotion to the Immaculate Conception and devotion to the poor souls originated, at least in this systematic form, simultaneously with the combined devotion to the Sacred Heart and the poor souls, in the second half of the 17th century by Sr. Mary-Margaret Alacoque.

It is clear that both manners of "suffrage" go together, as the Immaculate Heart of Our Lady is one with the Sacred Heart of her Son, and as it were directly animated by It. If her intercessory role with Him is so important for the living, why not also for the dead? Calling upon Our Lady as the Immaculate Conception—and by extension, as the Immaculate Heart, the one who has never been touched by sin—to help the souls in Purgatory must be according to the will of God. She who never had to expiate a sin herself became the most powerful Helper of those who have to. This is why Father Stanislaus called her "the most gracious Mother and the most merciful Protectress of the souls in purgatory."[1]

Significantly, a big canvas put up during the beatification ceremony depicted supplicating hands stretched out from the flames to a rosary above them. The souls crave this prayer. Calling upon the Blessed Virgin by praying the Rosary must be considered a most efficacious means to acquire her intercession on their behalf with the Holy Trinity. (The Rosary is ultimately a Trinitarian prayer, as Sister Lucia of Fatima has repeatedly pointed out.)

According to his own words, the divine inspiration that had urged Father Papczynski to found the Marian Congregation[2] implied the special task of this congregation to assist the suffering souls. "I promise," he wrote in his testament of 1692, "a double reward at God's hands to all those who choose and support this small Congregation of the Immaculate Conception, *brought into being by God to assist the dead.*"[3]

And Father Stanislaus gave the good example. He offered all of his good works, heroic prayers, and acts of penitence and all of his manifold physical, mental, and moral sufferings for the benefit of his brothers and sisters in Purgatory. "When (at the end of his life) his suffering intensified, he would say, as was his custom: 'Increase, O Lord, my suffering, that You may diminish the punishment of the souls in purgatory.'"[4] He was a miracle worker, too, but that was not why he was a great saint. This honor he deserved by his heroic charity for all the needy, for the priests, for the poor, and especially for the poor souls. He formed his confreres in the same spirit but fervently preached the devotion to the suffering souls to the laity as well and made it an essential part of the Marian spirituality of those who joined his lay Confraternity of the Immaculate Conception.

"The holy Mass of Father Stanislaus Papczynski." Painting by Father Jan Niez-abitowski, end of the 18th century, in the chapel of the Marian Fathers in Skórzec.

His generous love for the suffering souls was enormously impelled by his mystical visions of Purgatory. "His confreres and his other contemporaries were convinced that whenever he fell into ecstasy, he always had visions of purgatory. . . . During his long prayers that sometimes lasted all night, he would descend in spirit into purgatory and stay with the sufferings souls there."[5] The suffering he witnessed in that place or state, and which he sometimes shared in a mystical way, moved him profoundly and enkindled and sustained his zeal to sacrifice everything for them.

Father Papczynski's calling as a helper of the souls in Purgatory was providential. It came at a moment when many people in Poland were dying unprepared, by famine, natural disasters, epidemics, and continuous wars with the invading Turks and Swedes. Trustworthy evidence exists of at least several of his visits or visions of Purgatory. As a chaplain of the Polish army under King John III Sobieski[6] during the war with the Turks in the Ukraine in the spring of 1675, he prayed intensely at the graves of the soldiers and it seems that "many fallen soldiers appeared to him and asked his intercession before God."[7] This episode gave him the impetus to call on his beginning religious community to pray and make sacrifices for the dead, especially for the victims of war and epidemics.

Another story concerns Father Papczynski's visit to Purgatory, when he stayed at the court of the Polish noble Jacob Karski

> on occasion of the death of Mr. Karski's parents. After a service at the parish church and before a meal had begun, Father Stanislaus fell into ecstasy during which, as he confessed later, he watched the suffering souls in purgatory. . . . When he came to after a while, he rose from the table and without a word turned towards the door. He went straight to his monastery and said to his confreres, surprised by his unexpected return: "Pray, brethren, for the souls in purgatory, for they suffer unbearably!" Then he locked himself up in his cell for a few days without food or drink and prayed ardently for the souls suffering in purgatory.

Later, he confided this to Mr. Karski, who wanted an explanation of his remarkable behavior.[8]

In 1676 he made a pilgrimage to the shrine of Our Lady in Studzianna:

He fell gravely ill then and asked to be taken to the icon of the Holy Family, famous for miracles. At that time, Father John Ligeza, Father Stanislaus's close friend and confessor, was the superior of the Oratorian monastery in Studzianna. After confession and holy Mass, Father Stanislaus went to the cell assigned to him. There, he felt he was losing all his strength and senses. Half dead, in ecstasy, he once again experienced the mystery of the suffering souls in purgatory. As he watched this tremendous suffering, he felt that the Blessed Virgin was asking, together with all the souls, that he might return to life to help the dead.

While Father Stanislaus was in ecstasy, the residents of the monastery, having finished their dinner, came to his cell to see what was happening to him. They thought he was dead and informed Father Ligeza about it. They were already wondering what arrangements ought to be made for his funeral. But their superior was not alarmed by this news and assured them that Father Stanislaus had not died. He said that he knew where Father Stanislaus was. Soon afterwards, Father Papczynski returned to life and, having received the Superior's blessing, emaciated by the fever, went to the church and delivered a long sermon to a crowd of the faithful about the need to help the souls suffering in purgatory. Then he returned to his monastery and ordered his confreres to pray the rosary and say the Office of the Dead every day. He also told them to offer any merits, labors, fasts, mortifications, and other pious works for these souls, so that they might be freed from their unbearable punishments.[9]

This Sudzianna experience especially deserves more than a cursory look, because there is more in it than immediately catches the eye. The Blessed Virgin asks for his cure, together with the suffering souls, so that he may continue helping them. That logically implies that the souls, who cannot pray directly for themselves, do pray for the living who have mercy on them, so they are allowed to *indirectly* pray for themselves. It is also evident that the Mother of God herself supports this kind of prayer by them and pleads at the same time for them as well as for the living who help them. She is in fact seen by Father Stanislaus as functioning in her role of the interceding Mother of Christ at the Cana wedding, praying here for the dead and the living alike.

The Studzianna vision sheds further light on Father Papczynski's insistent counsel to pray the Rosary for the dead. Our Lady is asked to intercede for the souls, with a built-in beneficial effect for the faithful themselves who pray this favorite Marian prayer.

Secondly, Papczynski's doctrine emphasizes the atoning value of all mortifications and "labors." God's mercy for the poor souls accepts any effort of the living performed with the right intention as (partial) down payment for their debt. In consequence, the faithful can also offer the merits of the efforts he makes in his daily work for the souls in Purgatory.

And then we realize that a saint like Father Papczynski does not exaggerate out of lust of sensation or whatever impure motive when he enjoins on his hearers that the souls in Purgatory suffer "unbearably." He was an honest and conscientious preacher of the truth as it was, no more, no less. His beatification in this 21st century, which seems to have immunized itself against the great, serious realities of the "four last things" he always called attention to, is a reminder to the modern mind of the timeless urgency of his preaching.

"Father Stanislaus Papczynski comes to the aid of the souls in purgatory." Painting by Jan Niezabitowski in the rafter of the Marian Fathers in Skórzec.

CHAPTER 13

THE MODERN-DAY APPARITIONS
TO EUGENIE VON DER LEYEN

*A*pparitions from Purgatory share certain common features, no matter in which era the apparition takes place or to which person. Yet every individual apparition has its unique characteristics, too, and is instructive in its own way because it deepens our understanding of certain aspects of sin, atonement, and holiness.

While avoiding the two extremes of, on the one hand, taking the descriptions of apparitions after a too "fundamentalist" fashion, forgetting that the supernatural exceeds our concepts and images, and on the other hand, belittling them as "theologically unscientific" manifestations of a primitive, culturally determined, obsolete piety—the latter error is the predominant one in our time—we can learn a lot from trustworthy reports and documents. After all, insofar as their authenticity can be vouched for, they are messages from Heaven; God ordained them, so it would be reckless on our part to ignore them.[1]

A marvelous lesson that is especially implicit in the reports of "serial apparitions" of poor souls to their generous helpers concerns the beneficial effect of the charity done to them by the living; these stories graphically illustrate how the suffering souls gradually rise from their tormenting state, often until the point that they may enter eternal bliss.

The examples in this and the next chapters are drawn from reports of apparitions from the 20th century, because for the modern reader, stories of more recent apparitions are more interesting, and perhaps more acceptable, than similar stories of a more remote past. Moreover, they can exemplify both the constant, timeless elements in the way the souls manifest themselves and the wide individual variation of the intensity and kind of purification they live. Some are "severe cases," others "mild" ones. Some suffer in Purgatory for a short time, some for decades, others for centuries. The seers can all be regarded as saintly persons, but mostly they are not canonized saints.

We begin with some highlights from two serial apparitions to Eugenie von der Leyen (1867–1929), quoting her diary notes.

Eugenie was a cheerful, affectionate, generous, modest, and realistic woman. Everyone liked her, especially the children. The von der Leyens were of high German nobility, and Eugenie, who bore the title of princess, lived in the ancestral castle at Waal (Bavaria). By order of her confessor, she kept a sober and matter-of-fact diary of her contacts with the poor souls, which after her death was handed over to Eugenio Pacelli, the later Pope Pius XII, who was a learned mysticism expert and a good friend of the family.

THE MURDERED SHEPHERD FRITZ[2]

This apparition was preceded by some nights of "paranormal" tumults in the house:

June 11, 1923. At awakening, a long grayish form over me, completely nebulous; I can't say whether man or woman, but unsympathetic; am very frightened.

June 14. The phantom was already in my room when I wanted to sleep. Then I said my evening-prayer aloud, during which it came very near to me. If it hadn't been for his arms, it rather would seem a walking tree-trunk. It stayed perhaps twenty minutes, then came back at four o'clock.

June 16. It was very bad. It shook my shoulder. That is a horrible moment. I struck him and said: "You may not touch me!" Whereupon it withdrew in a corner. At my push, I didn't feel a body, it was like a humid, warm towel.[3] I believed I couldn't stand such terror any longer.

June 18. Again this horrible thing; it wanted to clasp my neck. I prayed in fear and took the particle of the Cross [a holy relic she possessed] in my hand. Then it remained with me, staying upright and big before me. It didn't answer questions;[4] then it went out through the door, which it left open.

June 19. I can recognize now that it is a man; [he] was only there for a short while.

June 21. The horrible man more than an hour during the night, went back and forth continuously. He has disheveled black hair and horrific eyes.

June 22. This man from one o'clock until past five with me, it was very bad. He repeatedly bowed over me and sat down at my bedside. I really wept for fear, then prayed the "hours" so that I didn't need to see him. Then he went again back and forth and moaned horribly. Now it seems to me I must know him, however I cannot find out who it is. I have become very cowardly, for many times it is really a decision for me to go to my room in the evening. Yet ordinarily I am able to fall asleep very well.

June 24. He came back, seized me at my shoulder. I said: "Now tell me what you want and then don't come back."[5] No answer; he went again through the room a couple of times and then was gone. My rest however was completely destroyed. At six in the morning he came back. In daylight he even looks more horrific, makes a disgusting impression, belongs to the dirtiest category of ghosts who have already come. I said: "Don't disturb me, I want to prepare myself for holy Communion!" Then he drew very near to me and lifted his hands imploringly. I was so sorry for him that I promised him a lot. Then I said: "Can't you speak?" Whereupon he shook his head. "Do you have much to suffer?" Now he moaned terribly. I gave him much holy water[6] and then he was gone.

June 27. He was there again, in the night. Seems to know me; I racked my brains as to who he might be. He is very unsympathetic.[7]

June 29. He was again in the room when I went to bed. It could be the murdered shepherd Fritz. I asked him at once, but he didn't react. I prayed with him, during which he fixed his eyes on me so angrily that I was really frightened. I asked him to go and then he went indeed.

June 30. He came very briefly; his moaning waked me up.

July 1. Again, [I] really believe it is shepherd Fritz. However his face is so black that I have difficulty recognizing him. But figure, nose, and eyes are wholly "he," as I saw him so many times in life.

July 2. He came back, didn't look so terribly wild anymore and stayed not for a long time. I addressed him as "shepherd Fritz," which he apparently found quite natural.

July 3. He came very briefly. I asked: "Are you the murdered shepherd Fritz?" Then he said distinctly: "Yes!"

July 4. He came to me in the morning, looked sadly at me and went away soon, answered nothing, too.

July 5. Now it struck me that everything about him is clearer. During prayer, he made the Sign of the Cross.

July 6. I am very happy for he can speak now. I asked him: "Why do you always come to me?" He: "Because you have always prayed for me." (That is right, for I had always been sorry for the poor fellow; he always looked so particular, even as a boy.) I: "Then what saved you?" He: "Insight and repentance."[8] I: "Weren't you dead immediately?" He: "No." I: "Will you be released soon?" He: "Not by far." Then I gave him permission to continue coming to me, if it does him well. How remarkable it is, that someone who was so rude in life speaks like that when separated from his body. Now I am not frightened by him anymore, and would like to help him as best I can. How merciful is the good Lord!

Father Sebastian Wieser, Eugenie's parish priest and confessor, comments:

> The behavior of this apparition is like the echo of his earthly life. I have known shepherd Fritz well—he was a "goat" in the parish. In him, the greatness of the mercy of God really manifests itself. Rarely he showed up in church. He had an only son, who already in school was conspicuous for his meanness, falsehood, and mendacity and caused many troubles to his teachers and those placed above him. When the boy had to be punished at school, the father pulled out all the stops of his indignation over schoolmaster and priest. I prophesied that the time would come that he would get a beating from this only son!
>
> When this son was seventeen years old, big and strong, he beat his father to death, at midnight. . . . Nobody knew if [Fritz] was dead immediately or if he came to for a moment. The latter seems to have been the case. The murderer has knocked him down in the hay-barn and abandoned him to his fate. Only in the morning was the dead man discovered. . . . On the sixth of July he tells that . . . "insight and repentance" have saved him from damnation! On the twelfth of July he says, "I am burning!" and presses a finger on the hand of the princess, which leaves a red burn which I have seen myself.

July 8. He came very briefly.

July 9. He came at six o'clock and so woke me up. Otherwise I had overslept. I: "Is it so important for you that I go to holy Mass?" He: "That way, you can help me a lot."

July 11. Only very briefly.

July 12. We prayed together,[9] then I: "Then what do you have to suffer?" He: "I am burning!" Then he came up to me and before I could defend myself, he pressed a finger on my hand. I was frightened so much and it hurt me so much, that I screamed. Now I have a red burn which I hope will heal soon. It is a very strange feeling, to have this visible mark from the other world.[10]

July 24. Shepherd Fritz and the other one [a new apparition] came two times in the night, all silent, but not very pleasant.

July 29. Nothing special to mention. Now these two are coming every night. The new one looks horrible, shepherd Fritz becomes ever more bright.[11]

August 10. Shepherd Fritz drew so near to me again, but looked very friendly.[12] So I said to him, "Don't you have to suffer so much anymore?" He: "No." I: "Can you pray for me yet?" He: "No." I: "Where are you then all the time?" He: "In the forlornness." I: "Will you still come often to me?" He: "No." I: "Why not?" He: "I am not allowed any more!"[13] I: "Have I been able to help you?" He: "Yes." Then he was gone.

August 11. Came G . . . four times in the night. Actually I am sad that shepherd Fritz doesn't come again. . . .[14] In general, my nerves must be much better; I've gotten altogether used to the uninvited guests and can sleep very well afterwards.

OLD HEINZ[15]

November 15. I saw for the first time the old Heinz in the garden; he looks terrible.

November 21. Heinz was there for a very long time, restless and looking angry. He whines continuously; praying makes him even more restless, I would almost say more angry. At dawn, Katharina came [another poor soul, who had died in 1680; long ago!]. It felt very agreeable not to be alone with Heinz. Now she began by herself her lovely prayer,[16] so that I had to weep. . . . Heinz stood by. The difference between the two is great, like [between] shadow and light, like anger and meekness.

November 22. Both were here again. Heinz abhors prayer, which is plain to see on his face. But I don't care about it; I pray all the same.[17]

November 25. Heinz there alone. He was so wild that I thought he might even fall in my bath tub.[18] I said: "Do you have to tell me something?" Then he grew totally wild, ran away, came back again and moaned terribly. . . . [19] It was not pleasant.

November 29. Only Heinz there. Praying and questioning irritates him.

December 1. Very unpleasant night. Old Heinz was there for a long time and very horrific. I asked if he had shot at my grandfather at that time [there had been an—apparently fatal—attempt on her grandfather's life]. That made him furious. Before I could resist, he threw himself upon me and strangled me so firmly by my neck that I thought I would suffocate. It didn't last more than a second, to be sure, but it was horrible and totally upset me. I shall never forget these furious eyes.[20] At each of these incidents of being touched by ghosts (three, until now) I have more a feeling of disgust than of pain, as if I had to touch a toad or a snake.

December 2. He was with me from 2-6 o'clock; he was so obtrusive that I could hardly defend myself. I held the particle of the Cross before him, then he screamed and withdrew in a corner,[21] where he then stayed like an angrily growling dog. It was very bad.

December 3. At first came Heinz and then Katharina. I asked them: "Don't you still see the other ghost?" They: "No." I: "Why not?" She: "This circle has been overcome." I: "Please tell me if it is an angry ghost." She: "Save him.". . . Heinz was quiet but horrible.

A short aside. "This circle has been overcome." Purgatory, or the purifying process, is likely to go through stages. According to the statements of some souls to princess Eugenie there is a "lowest stage" for the souls that are "saved, not yet purified"; some souls—they seem "beautiful and peaceful"—dwell in "a higher sphere," are no more ablaze in a fire but dwell in a "space in-between, between darkness and clarity," where they are already happy (in a certain sense), but still ardently longing for God.[22] Probably, the traditional distinction between the pain of the senses and the pain of loss is indicated by this.

"December 4. Heinz here in the night, prayed with him, which is altogether indifferent to him. It strikes me ever more how dark the

phantoms initially are in their face; actually, it clarifies only when they can speak.[23]

December 6. Heinz there almost half of the night. The particle of the Cross is my protection; now he doesn't come so near to me.

December 8. Heinz was furious. He threw himself on the floor. I prayed to the Mother of God, and he became a little bit more quiet. These prayers of mine are very inattentive, however, pure lip-prayer, for my whole thinking is preoccupied with the phantom, which I do not lose out of sight, for fear.[24] At three o'clock in the night he went away, to return at five. "Go away! I will go to church; there I can pray better for you." Then he screamed horribly. So I prayed again with him; then he sobbed so badly that I wanted to say something nice to him. Then it crossed my mind that when I was a child he had more than once handed me some prunes over the fence. So I said to him: "I thank you as yet that you often did me a pleasure. I didn't forget it. Just tell me how I can help you. I do it with pleasure."[25] There came a gargling sound and he reached out his hand to me. I took it; it was hot. Then his face turned more friendly, if one may call it so, for he is very repulsive. I said: "Now go away; I must go to the church," and he went away. Now our friendship is established, I believe, because as soon as I can show love instead of fear, it becomes better.

December 12. Heinz there a long time, a bit better, also seems not hostile to prayer any more.

December 18. When I returned, Heinz was in my room. I: "Have just prayed for you a lot; tell me what you want!" He: "Forgiveness!" I: "Did you fire at my grandfather?" He: "Instigated, slandered!" I: "I have to ask you: Were you ill or possessed?" He: "Possessed." I: "By whom?" He: "Spirit of lying." All this he said in a whining voice and he looked pitiful. I am so happy that he finally speaks. (It actually seems an injustice to me that I uncover the faults of the poor ones, like a loveless breach of confidence; obedience and charity are somehow in conflict within me.)

Vicar Sebastian Wieser writes,

I knew the Heinz as well as Fritz the Shepherd and others. He lived across from my house and I visited him rather often in the days when he was mentally clouded. The shot hole is shown still today. Heinz died about fifty years ago. Now he confesses that he has been the instigator of the fatal shot, and answers to the question I had occasioned, whether he was mentally ill or possessed, that he had been possessed by the spirit of lying. The reason I tried to ask this question is this: I am of the opinion that a large part of "crazy" people are possessed.[26]

December 19. At dawn came Heinz. I: "Do you want to pray with me?" He: "Yes." I: "Does it relieve you?" He: "Yes." I: "Why did you strangle me then, a short time ago?" He: "In torment!"[27] I: "Won't you do it again?" He: "No!" I: "Why don't you go, then, to your relatives?" He: "No way to them!" During prayer, he is very much different, now.

December 24. Heinz with me for a long time; he looks better. I: "Are you doing better?" He: "Yes." I: "Are you released soon?" He: "Eighteen times seven." I: "Tell me, if there are other souls with me that I cannot yet see?" He: "Yes." I: "Why can't I see them?" He: "They are not permitted." Then he was gone.

December 28. Heinz here. Since he looked so sad, I asked him why. He: "You didn't give me anything." I: "Pardon me, I know I have neglected you, because I feel also so sorry for the other ones; I shall take care of you first, now."

December 29. Heinz here; I asked many things, got no answer. He has prayed eagerly and when I gave him holy water, he kept altogether quiet.

December 30. Heinz a very long time there. Whichever prayer I began, he was always dissatisfied, expressing it in moaning and unrest. Finally [the *Memorare*] came to my mind, then he was quiet. It occurred to me that, surely, the Mother of God had saved him. So I said: "How have you been saved?" No answer. I: "I want to know!" He: "Mother of . . . cy" (no doubt "Mercy," was not understandable). I: "Did you always venerate her?" He: "Yes." Such communications are always heart-warming and I was very happy. How many similar questions I had asked already, without getting an answer.[28]

January 4, 1924. Afterwards came Heinz. I: "Are you content with me now?" He: "Yes." I: "Should I do everything for you, nothing for the others?" He: "Give me more!" How he sees through me; because, actually, I could give more, if I were not just "I"!

January 10. Heinz came in full daylight; he looked content. I: "You just look very content, are you going better?" He: "Yes." I: "Just tell me how it is that you still have to expiate. For I have offered up for you so many times a plenary indulgence, haven't I?" He: "Yes." I: "Have you experienced it?' He: "Yes, God is just, the torment ceases, the punishment doesn't!" Then he was gone.

January 11. Heinz here almost the whole night. Now he really looks very content. I: "Just tell me, why have you been possessed?" He: "Giving scandal!"[29] I: "Where are you now?" He: "In the shadow!" I: "Still far from the good God?" He: "Yes." I: "Shall you come often to me?" He: "No." I: "Why not?" He: "You cannot give me anything anymore." I: "But I help you with pleasure, all the same." He: "I am released!" I: "What do you have to suffer as yet?" He: "The punishment of deprivation!" Then he was gone. How wonderful, all of this. I only write down what I can hear with certainty. For many times I must ask repeatedly, as they often mumble so much.

Eugenie was one of those strong, generous souls who in the history of Catholicism have always been called to holiness by doing penance, especially for the apparently "severe cases" in the abode of purification. To her came suffering souls that had been in Purgatory for very long periods, others who had led a bad life and, had they not been saved at the last moment by God's mercy, would have gone to Hell (but then, the process of their expiation was very hard). That is an encouraging reality, which reminds us of similar cases reported in the life of the Curé of Ars.

Her diary entries show how exhausting this work of mercy can be and that the more she gave herself to the poor souls, the more there were who desperately clung to her and pressed her to give everything she had. If we realize that God is behind all apparitions of souls, the conclusion must be that He is so eager to release the suffering souls that He allowed them nearly to force the seer to consume her powers in their service. But from her diary it also transpires that she herself became more holy, more purified, selfless, in the process; God's grace is multifunctional. And it evidences the spiritual help she received from above and the mystical joys she would experience at the end of her life.

CHAPTER 14

A DECEASED SISTER VISITS ST. FAUSTINA

Within two months, the sacrifices of Eugenie von der Leyen had carried both Fritz and old Heinz out of the pit of their torments into a state of contentment and peace. That must have been the limit God's justice had, so to speak, put to His mercy; Jesus Himself had hinted at the requirements of His justice as "opposed" to His mercy when He spoke to St. Faustina these beautiful, moving words on Purgatory: "My mercy does not want this, but justice demands it."[1] Old Heinz was aware of it—witness his remark, full of abandonment to God's adorable will: "God is just, the torment is finished, not the punishment." Still "far" from God, he suggested that he had to suffer for a long time the pain of unfulfilled desire for God.

Fortunately, many other souls—Eugenie's experiences comprised a few of these cases too, and many others are encountered in the stories about other famous helpers of the poor souls, such as Maria Anna Lindmayr, or the Blessed Sister Anne Catherine Emmerick (1774–1824)—can be helped straight to Heaven. At times, one may get the impression that they seem to belong to a class of "milder cases." An example is the soul of the deceased Sister who belonged to the same congregation as St. Faustina, to whom she appeared shortly after her death.

It happened probably only a few weeks after the guardian angel of this (recently canonized) saint had taken her to Purgatory—it was at the start of her monastic life—where she was told that the greatest suffering of the soul is its longing for God. That journey was apparently intended to imprint on her soul the need to carry the mercy of Christ not only to this world but also no less to the next.

Significantly, Sister Faustina wrote that "since that time, I am in closer communion with the suffering souls,"[2] and she was to stay that way.

On April 29, 1926, Faustina's diary reads, "A Sister [Henry] was dying. A few days later she came to me and bid me to go to Mother Directress of Novices . . . and tell her to ask her confessor . . . to offer one Mass for her and three ejaculatory prayers. At first I agreed, but

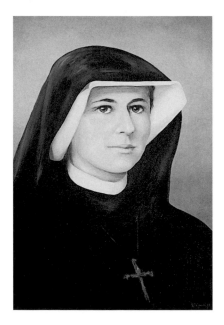

St. Faustina Kowalska: "Since that time, I am in closer communion with the suffering souls".

the next day I decided I would not go to Mother Directress, because I was not sure whether this had happened in a dream or in reality. And so I did not go."

Every mentally normal person will probably doubt himself when faced for the first time with the speaking ghost of a departed person, and will be inclined to decide it must have been an illusion. This was certainly the case for 21-year-old Sister Faustina, who evidenced no sign of overexcitement. The continuation of the story indicates again a healthy critical attitude:

> The following night the same thing was repeated more clearly; I had no more doubt. Still, in the morning[3] I decided not to tell the Directress about it unless I saw her [Sister Henry] during the day. At once I ran into her in the corridor. She reproached me for not having gone immediately, and a great uneasiness filled my soul. So I went immediately to Mother Directress and told her everything that had happened to me. Mother responded that she would take care of the matter. At once peace reigned in my soul, and on the third day this sister came to me and said, "May God repay you."

Sister Faustina (along with Padre Pio) represents the modern *canonized* saints who have distinguished themselves as helpers of the poor souls. One cannot expect it to be otherwise. How could a saintly person, who has made much progress on the way to perfection because of his love of God and neighbor, not be more than on average charitable to the dead? St. Faustina was called to be the modern apostle of Divine Mercy. It is a good thing, therefore, to realize that her apostolate included, logically enough, providing a good example to our age on being merciful to the suffering souls in Purgatory.

CHAPTER 15

URSULA HIBBELN: THE SIMPLE
WOMAN WHO HELPED MANY SOULS

*T*he case of Ursula Hibbeln (1869–1940), a simple, inconspicuous labor-class woman living in the German industrial *Ruhrge-biet*, may stand for many more similar cases of unknown saints who have sacrificed themselves for the suffering souls. Even after their death, they are known only in a very limited circle and for a limited period.[1]

Ursula Hibbeln's contact with the poor souls has been examined by several competent priests.[2] Her spiritual director persisted for ten years in treating the apparitions as "delusions," but in view of the many cases where he could substantiate the information given her by the deceased, he had to change his mind. Ursula suffered from serious physical illnesses, but never complained, and is described by those who knew her as "really humane, full of love and gladness and joy," "of a charming naturalness and captivating," "full of understanding," without "a shade of pride," and in her communications "always simple and matter-of-fact."[3] Very pious, she had a "boundless confidence in God," and "her whole longing was to save all souls for God." Already as a child she'd had apparitions of poor souls, for whom she prayed fervently and offered up many mortifications.

Most souls appearing to her did not seem to find themselves in the condition of utter misery we saw in a few who came to Eugenie von der Leyen, but some were nonetheless very long in Purgatory.[4] Ursula once said that there are many who must stay in Purgatory until the end of the world[5]—the case of Amélia from Fatima[6] apparently does not stand alone. (By the way, the English Benedictine monk St. Bede [673–735] had stated the same, so the idea has a respectable tradition.)

As in times long past, souls appeared to her in different forms, either just as they had been in their life, or more or less symbolic: a man who had committed suicide by a shot in the mouth showed up more than once, holding the revolver in his mouth, while fire came out of his mouth. A woman who had died a couple of days before appeared with wide-opened, frightened eyes. She had never imagined that Purgatory was like it was and begged most insistently to tell her family to pray much for her. She had to remain a year in Purgatory. Despite having led a good life, she had been very egoistic and loveless to her husband and children.[7]

Ursula Hibbeln also saw many deceased persons she had never known. Obviously, apart from having to do penance herself for these souls, she also had to be the channel for transmitting the urgent requests of these souls for help to their family. (One might wonder whether this grace would not be conferred more frequently on family members of a deceased person if the devotion to the poor souls were practiced more zealously.)

Of course, this is not to be confused with the kind of deceptive, occult "channeling" or spiritualist contact with the dead of so many "paranormals," "psychics," or allegedly telepathic "seers." The latter class of persons have no contact with the real dead at all; their dabbling in the occult is rather an invitation to the demons.

True seers like Ursula do not raise up spirits themselves; they are called by God to receive them and to sacrifice themselves for them. Therefore, they receive the love, strength, and courage to cope with the harsh reality of Purgatory. This lesson was once taught to Ursula's husband, who, understandably enough, doubted whether his wife was really visited so continuously by poor souls. One day he asked his wife to show him one such soul. Ursula prayed for that grace, and shortly afterward, a soul came to him. This frightened him so much that he exclaimed, "Never more in my life the vision of a poor soul!"[8]

* * *

The view of the "last things" transmitted by Ursula's apparitions is as serious and profound as it has been since early Christianity. Purgatory indeed means burning, however mystical that fire may be.

A relative was a Freemason, yet shortly before his death he had the grace to receive the Sacraments of the dying. Mrs. Hibbeln said, "He is saved. He is in the place in purgatory where the flames cannot break out, in the deepest pool of flames." Once I asked, "The soul is a spirit, isn't it, and cannot suffer the pains of burning?" She answered, "Pain of burning is only felt through the nerves in the brain; so it is in purgatory, too. The soul feels the pain as if still united with the body. If the person has sinned with his hands, then the soul has the pain as if the hands are put in the flames; so it happens with every member of the body that has sinned."[9]

Hibbeln also had joyful communications. "Father and mother are in heaven," she could tell a visitor whose parents had died.[10] Or, to a young widow whose husband was killed in an accident and who was very much concerned about his salvation: "He still lived three hours [after the accident] and prepared himself for death." He was released after a year.[11] His death is reminiscent of the death of the murdered Fritz who appeared to Eugenie von der Leyen.[12]

A woman whose husband had been a Freemason was enormously consoled when Ursula told her that the man had met with God's mercy and was saved because she had done much good,[13] an example that implies practical advice to those married whose partner does not live well and gives them hope at the same time!

Ursula Hibbeln exemplifies how God seeks His helpers from all educational levels and social classes, and her case suggests, like that of the Bohemian farmer's wife, who we shall meet in chapter 17, that probably more ordinary lay people than we shall ever know (here on earth) belong to this chosen category. There are *incognito* saints within the Catholic community, whose self-denial and charity may be sensed—to a degree—by their environment but is still, for the most, part hidden in an ordinary daily life or in the silence of the heroism with which they suffer. However, saintly priest or monastic, princess, farmer, or labor-class woman as *Frau* Hibbeln, the communications they receive from the poor souls who visit them and their profound insights into Purgatory do not differ.

CHAPTER 16

TWO APPARITIONS TO PADRE PIO

S aint Padre Pio (1887–1968), the Capuchin monk who made San Giovanni Rotondo famous, needs no introduction. It is, however, less known that among the multitude of his visitors, so many came from Purgatory. Not surprising, considering this saint's life of heroic sacrifices for the salvation of all souls and for all of their other needs.

Father Joseph Pius Martin, who had shared daily life with Padre Pio for a long time as his personal caretaker, had this to say:[1]

> You know how many people visited Padre Pio each day—every year? Well, Padre Pio once said that there were more souls of the dead who come up that road [the road leading to the monastery] then souls of the living. The stories about these departed souls are fantastic. One day a car with three or four Capuchins over-turned in northern Italy and all were killed. The Capuchins at San Giovanni Rotondo told Padre Pio what had happened, and they asked for his prayers. But it seems quite clear from his reactions that he had already known that they were dead. Evidently he had seen them at night.

Padre Pio from Pietrelcina was more often visited by souls from Purgatory.

When the Church took away some indulgences, he was surprised. He said, "Now who will think of the Holy Souls? Pray hard for them every day."[2] He was in frequent conversation with them. I am quite sure that certain people who died were permitted to go to Padre Pio and request certain things for their families.

Also Father Raffaele, who lived with Padre Pio in the monastery for thirty-five years, during thirteen of which he was his Superior. He told the following two stories, which unmistakably bear the hallmarks of Padre Pio's common sense and directness and a touch of his typical humor.[3]

THE DEAD MAN

It happened around 1918 or 1919 . . . Assunta, the sister of Padre Paolino, had come to visit her brother. In the evening, since the hour was late and her room was far away, she occupied a small room in the guest quarters of the friary. After supper, Padre Paolino said to Padre Pio, "Let's go and say hello to Assunta in the guest quarters."

While they visited with her, Padre Pio became very drowsy and sat down next to the fireplace. It was November, and it was quite cold. Seeing Padre Pio so tired, Padre Paolino said to him, "We are going to pay a visit to the Blessed Sacrament. In the meanwhile, you stay here and rest, because you are so tired." Padre Pio agreed, and Paolino and his sister went into the church through the sacristy. Before long Padre Pio fell into a light sleep. Suddenly he woke up. He opened his eyes and saw an old man bundled up in a heavy overcoat, warming his hands by the fire. He said to the old man, "Who are you? What are you doing here?" The old man replied, "'I am so-and-so.'"

Padre Pio said, "What are you doing here?" He answered: "I am in Purgatory to atone for this and this."

Padre Pio said, "Well, I'm talking to you now, and we will not talk about this any more. Tomorrow morning I will offer a Mass for you and you will be liberated, but don't you come here any more."

He took the old man by the arm and walked outside with him as far as the tree. . . . Padre Pio said to the old man, "Don't come back here any more." He said goodbye to the old man, and the old man disappeared. . . . Remember that when Padre Pio had walked outside, the door remained locked, because when he came back, he found the door locked and bolted. So he rang the bell. Padre Paolino opened the door and asked, "What are you doing outside? How did you get out here?" Padre Pio answered, "I had to go to the bathroom." Padre Paolino said, "Don't hand me that story. It is not true, because the door was locked." Padre Pio said, "No, no, the door was open." Paolino said: "No, the door was locked." The debate went back and forth.[4] After a few days Padre Pio said, "I said that the door was open because I didn't want to explain what really happened."

For several days Padre Pio did not look well. He was very pensive and sad and pale. Padre Paolino asked him several times, "What happened that night? Don't you feel well? Are you sick?" At first Padre Pio would not say anything. Finally he told Paolino what had actually happened concerning the old man.

The next day Padre Pio sent Paolino to the city hall to find out about this old man who had died—to learn his name and when and where he had died. They told him, "Yes, there was an old man who had died at the friary. He was burned alive in room number four. His name was something like Preconci. At that time the friary was a home for the poor. The poor used room number four. This man used to smoke a lot in bed. One night in 1886 this man set his bed on fire and was burned alive." I have no doubt that Padre Pio had spoken to this dead man from San Giovanni Rotondo. That is story one.

So this soul was about 32 years in Purgatory. One might speculate if he was one of those who "go about" the place where they lived or died, waiting for a person who can help them (i.e., to whom God wants to send them and have them appear). Did he warm his hands to express he was in want of something—a silent appeal to Padre Pio to help him? Or was it simply what he had often done in his life? Or both?

THE BROKEN CANDLES

Now I want to tell you another story that happened in the church. Every evening after supper all the friars used to come together for a common recreation, and Padre Pio would go with them. Then Padre Pio would go to the oratory and pray by himself.

One evening as Padre Pio was all by himself praying in the oratory, he heard a noise in the church. He thought, *It must be the students—the boys who are straightening things up in the church*. So he didn't pay any further attention to the incident.

There were candles all around the altar. You would have to use a ladder to get to them. As Padre Pio was praying, he heard a noise like—*vroom*—and everything came crashing down. He got up from where he was and went to the Communion rail. He saw a young man dressed as a friar. The man was kneeling down. Padre Pio went up to him and said in a loud voice: "Eh, who are you?" The young man said: "I am a Capuchin novice, and I am from Purgatory, doing penance for the lack of diligence in my work in the church."

Padre Pio said, "Well, then! This is a fine way to make reparation—breaking up all the candles! Now listen to me. Go away, and don't you come here any more. Tomorrow my Mass will be for you. In this way you will be liberated. Never come back." The novice thanked him, and Padre Pio left the church. When Padre Pio realized that he had been speaking to a dead man, a cold shiver ran up and down his spine.

While this was happening, Padre Emmanuele was passing by. He said to Padre Pio, "Did you talk with a dead man? I was standing near the Communion rail and I realized that you were talking with a dead man. I got so scared I ran out. I went to get help." He returned with Padre Paolino. Padre Pio was shaking. He said, "I'm cold, I'm cold." Paolino asked him what had happened. He answered, "I was talking to a dead man." After about twenty minutes he said to Emmanuele, "Get a candle and come with me." They went into the church to the main altar. Padre Pio said, "Jump up on the altar."

He did. Then he asked, "Now what do you want me to do?" Padre Pio said, "Look behind the altar. Are there any broken candles there?" At the time the altar had a picture of St. Michael on it. He said, "Look under the picture of St. Michael behind the altar, and see if there are any broken candles." Emmanuele looked and said, "Yes, there are some large candles here. They are all broken. Now what else?"

Padre Pio said, "Now come down. That's enough. No more. Let's get out of here." And they walked out of the church.

Here the apparition left no burn mark, but another concrete, meaningful trace. The poor soul gave a demonstration of the negligent friar he had been and that way attracted Padre Pio's attention. He had to do penance where he had committed his fault.

CHAPTER 17

THE BOHEMIAN WIDOW
WHO SAW THE DEAD

A few examples of the doubtless many "discreet," inconspicuous apparitions of poor souls that do not get wider publicity (or remain virtually unknown) can be found in the memoirs of a modest German parish priest, Hermann Wagner. Wagner survived the Nazi years despite doing his duty as a priest amid many dangers.[1] It was in his parish in Flanitze (Bohemia, now the Czech Republic) that a humble widow confided to him that she was visited by souls from Purgatory. The souls had requested her to tell the priest about Purgatory in order for him to promote the devotion to them.

Ruth (pseudonym) was in her 50s at the time she got her first apparition. Her husband had died eight years before. Her only son had been killed during the German invasion of Poland. She had a small farmstead with two cows, usually a calf, and some pigs, and had to do all the work alone. She went almost daily to holy Mass, mostly in the company of children from the village. She was viewed as a quiet and pious person who did a lot of good. No one except this one parish priest ever knew of the coming of the poor souls to her.

The first was her departed husband. He had often been impatient during his bout with cancer and had reproached God.

One evening, Ruth heard a voice. [That happened] almost every evening, over a long time, when she came in from the stable. Then she suddenly recognizes the voice of her husband. But she isn't quite sure. Then she kneels down and just prays the Rosary for the poor souls. She recommends her husband in particular. Yes, she thinks, he was often rather impatient; is that perhaps the reason he must still do penance?

A few evenings later, she sees a nebulous apparition, right in the middle of the room.[2] She takes holy water and prays, "O Lord, give him eternal rest!" It makes her very upset. She wants to call the woman next door—is already on her way to the door. Then she sees her husband. He speaks quietly: "Don't be afraid, Ruth! It's me. I may come here to ask your help. Pray three chaplets each day.[3] And don't tell anybody. They wouldn't speak well of it!" Then he is gone.

Every day she prays three chaplets. Each time she adds, "Good God, forgive my husband his impatience when he suffered!" After some weeks, her husband stands again in the middle of the room. He looks well. He is friendly and beautiful. She recalls how he was as a young man. He says nothing. He only looks at her so grateful and full of love. Then she asks him, "How are you, Jacob?" He answers clearly and quietly, "I'm fine. I may come home soon. I thank you, Ruth! I thank you so much!" He looks at her really so sweet and thankful. Actually, like he never did in his life. Then he was always in a hurry. He never had time to say "thank you."

Ruth says she would like to give him a hand and embrace him. He makes a gesture of refusal and says, 'Later, Ruth. One day it shall be wonderful. Now I am allowed to tell you only one thing: there are others who also want to come to you. They have permission; God gave it to them. You can help them. Don't reject them! And don't be afraid! Never be afraid!" And gone he is! He never appeared again. She thinks he must already be in Heaven.

But no poor souls appear to her for a period of time. Then her only son, Jacob, is killed on the battlefield in Poland, and she begins to pray for them fervently. Now she prays very much for the poor souls, and always asks them how it is with her Jacob. She thinks the poor souls hear that, when she asks it so simply. For a long time, no answer.

Then unexpectedly, one afternoon when she is cleaning the room, an old woman appears. She looks very old and very wrinkled, ugly and frightening, like a gypsy. At first Ruth doesn't think it might be a poor soul. The woman doesn't say a word.

Then Ruth takes a closer look at her. *My God,* she thinks, *if she were not so ugly, she almost looks like my old grandma, on my mother's side.* Her name was Johanna, Grandma Johanna, dead so long already. Ruth asks, "Who are you then? I don't know who you are!" There the old woman answers[4] with a strange, eerie voice, "You do know me!" Ruth says, "If it were possible, I would say you are Grandma Johanna. But . . ." The old woman, still fixed to the door, replied, "Yes, that's me. Your grandma.[5]

Ruth is not particularly frightened. Her husband had told her she shouldn't be, when others would come. So she asks, "Well, dear grandma, tell me what I can do for you?" The old woman says, "You can do a lot for me. Pray every day a chaplet specially for me. And be really good for the poor. And when someone needs help." And vanished is the apparition at the door.

Ruth remembers that this grandmother was always very hard on others, that she had often scolded people, and that she hadn't liked praying either. Now Ruth prays every day another chaplet, and she goes to church every day, though it is not always easy, because, after all, she has to work in the stable. But she does it out of love for the poor souls. And it is never "No" to the poor or when someone needs help.

A few months later, Grandma Johanna appears again, this time not looking nearly as wrinkled or ugly. She even smiles.[6]

Ruth asks, "Dear grandma, how are you now? You look fine." Grandma nods smilingly: "I thank you, sweet Ruth! You have helped me very much. At first my way up was so terribly long and so full of stones that I almost despaired. Now it is not far anymore. I thank you, Ruth!" Already turned around halfway to go away, she looks back once more to Ruth, smiling, "You have always asked how it is with your son Jacob. You need not worry about him. This one is already altogether on high. He was lying a whole night in a shell crater, severely wounded. Then he called upon Jesus, if he might put his wounds in the wounds of Jesus. That way he died. His guardian angel was permitted to bring him up straight away. His death was a death of sacrifice, taking part of the sacrifice of Jesus. Dying is beautiful if you love Jesus." Ruth gets tears in her eyes at this good news. "Grandma, thank you so much for telling me this!" She wants to go to her grandmother, to shake hands with her, gratefully. But grandma keeps her at bay, lovingly: "You need not worry about me any more. But others will come. Don't be afraid!" Gone is she, never to appear again.

Eight days later, Ruth is feeding the pigs when she becomes suddenly aware of a man sitting at a table near her.

He is not old, but his looks are hard and embittered. He looks like a dangerous criminal, Ruth thinks. But this time she knows at once that he is a poor soul. And immediately she asks, "What do you want, then?" Then comes croaking out, as from a suffocated throat, "Help, help I need!" Ruth: "How can I help you?" Answer: "Be good, be good for people! Also for the cattle! Be good, think good, speak good, do good! Be good and give me whatever good you do!" He is gone. Ruth cannot remember ever seeing him in her life. He must be a complete stranger.

He needs the sacrifice of being good, Ruth believes, probably because he has been hard in his life and gave no love. Meanwhile, other souls are coming, too. They have their requests, all of them— still more prayers, still more sacrifices. She eats nothing but potatoes and sour milk. All the rest she gives away.[7] When she thinks she cannot do more, she notices that the poor souls accommodate her. No more of them are allowed to come than she can cope with.

She is very good, also, to the animals in the stable, and the effect is that the animals cling to her very much. She has a little calf of three months already, in perfect good health and attached to her. She considers keeping the calf and doing away with one of the older cows. Then she is visited by a far relative who admires the calf and expresses a need for it. Ruth thinks of the man with the hard face who appeared to her. She asks, "Do you want it, the calf?" He says that, at the moment, he cannot pay for it, but later, when things are going better. Ruth waves it aside: "It will be all right. Just take it with you!" The relative is overjoyed. He cannot thank her enough. But the little calf is gone. Will he ever pay for it? Is not important, she thinks. It is a good work, like the poor soul had demanded.

In the evening, just as Ruth rises after praying the Rosary, there he sits again at the table. He is not hard and embittered anymore. Rather, he looks like a good-natured and benevolent man. Ruth asks him, "Now, good man, are you satisfied with my goodness?" He rises and bows: "You helped me a lot with your good deed. All hard slugs have fallen from my heart.[8] Now I can already happily look upward. Up there, there is only love. Now my way isn't hopeless any more.[9] I thank you!" The seat where he was seated is empty. He never comes back.

* * *

Some souls expressed in their mode of appearance the sins they had to do penance for, as well as the nature of the penance—not unlike the young friar who appeared to Padre Pio. A young mother, with a face weathered and rugged from crying, appeared while looking desperately for her five children. She had neglected their religious education and now had to suffer from the terrible feeling that they were "lost" for eternity by her fault. Ruth gave satisfaction to God in her place by taking extra pains to give religious instruction to the children of the village. Appearing again after two months, the relieved woman declared that she was allowed to see her children from afar—curiously, they were still living on earth—and needed not be afraid of "losing" them anymore.

This humble seer had received much insight in the ways of Purgatory. "Most poor souls are never allowed to make themselves known by appearing to someone," she noted. "In particular not the poorest poor souls." Also Ruth affirmed that a certain category of poor souls do penance in such a terrible darkness and desolation that they believe they are lost forever. If such a soul were to appear, it would be unendurable; if a human being were to see their real condition, he would die.

She also learned that many proud souls go to Hell. If they are
saved, their Purgatory is enkindled by the humility and the love of
Christ. Initially, the humility of Christ works in them as an ineffable blaze of fire "that burns and burns until in the end all pride has
melted away." (Thus Ruth explains the fire of Purgatory as Catherine
of Genoa did.) The living can help these proud souls by offering up
humiliations for them. Ruth resembles St. Catherine and St. Faustina in her warnings to the living:

> Many are heading straight on for purgatory. They live until their
> last hour, even though they are seriously ill, even on their death-
> bed, as if everything is all right. Exclusively directed to the earthly,
> they don't think at all about calling upon the mercy of God.
> Although by doing so they would be spared at least a severe purga-
> tory. For God is infinitely merciful for all who call upon Him and
> trust Him.

According to Ruth—who stands here again in a strong, age-old
tradition—no one is as grateful as the poor souls. She emphasizes the
involvement of the guardian angels in the fate of the holy soul, in
general, and in rewarding its helper, in particular. Poor souls can help
us even if they are still in Purgatory. "They may help us through their
guardian angels.[10] They are allowed to help us often so effectively
that all of us can in fact notice it. We just should pay attention to it."
As for herself, according to Father Wagner, she

> need not be afraid of anything since she helps the poor souls. The
> guardian angels of the poor souls take care of everything. Just one
> example: [One day] she goes to church early in the morning, with
> a couple of kids. Two little boys and a little girl are still too young
> for that and may stay at home, in the room. As it is cold, she gives
> a blanket to the little girl, to wrap herself in. She has poked up
> the stove. As it often happens with little children, the two boys
> climb on the table, go hanging on the kerosene lamp above it and
> pull the lamp down. The lamp breaks. The kerosene is spreading
> on the floor. The lamp was already out, but the girl had installed
> herself so close to the stove that her blanket got singed. The girl

throws the red-hot blanket away, onto the floor. The kerosene flows to within a few centimeters from the red-hot blanket. That is how Ruth finds the children in the room when she comes home from the church. Immediately she throws the red-hot blanket out in the snow and straightens everything up. She knows that the holy angels of the poor souls have preserved the house from a fatal fire. She thanks them.

Poor souls told Ruth that they are often present around their living family members and beloved without getting their help, sometimes for years.[11] She transmits their complaints:

You in the world have no inkling of what we have to suffer! Being abandoned and forgotten by those who have been nearest to us in the world: that is most bitter. Sometimes they stand at the tombs of our decayed bodies and don't pray for us at all. They act as if we don't exist any more. God's justice commands us to be silent. But we stand at the door of their houses, of our former dwellings, and wait. We stand there and wait. Days, years. We wait for them to give us a small sign of their love by prayer and sacrifices. But we stay there in vain. We cry in vain for love. For help! Tell them through the priest:[12] Love should not die at death. We are still alive and we are *hungry for love!* For your love!

CHAPTER 18

HOW WE CAN
HELP THE HOLY SOULS

Since early Christianity there has been unanimity that offering the Sacrifice of the Altar to the holy Trinity is the most beneficial suffrage for the poor souls. Therefore, in the year 387, St. Monica, the mother of St. Augustine, asked her sons in her dying hour "only one thing: that you remember me at the altar of the Lord, wherever you shall be."[1] St. Thomas held that only by holy Mass could a soul be definitively delivered from Purgatory.[2] Poor souls indeed very often ask for holy Masses; but an expiatory act of high value is also the offering up of holy Communions, even of so-called spiritual communions. Furthermore, prayers, alms, indeed all acts of charity[3] and all and every ordinary daily work;[4] all mortifications and sacrifices that are offered to God for the relief or release of the suffering souls.

The significance of the link between the Sacred Heart of Jesus and these diverse forms of help to the souls in Purgatory—a link to which we have referred several times—is obvious. For the devotion to the Sacred Heart requires that the faithful unite all their activities with the Heart of Christ, which is perfectly present in the Eucharist, in order

St. Monica, mother of St. Augustine. At the hour of her death (in 387), she asked her sons "only one thing: that you remember me at the altar of the Lord, wherever you shall be." Statue by F. Jeracy, about 1900, in the church of Our Lady of Visitation, Warsaw.

to make them meritorious. That is what Our Lord had taught to St. Gertrude,[5] long before He appeared to St. Margaret Mary Alacoque; and the Blessed Claude de la Colombière, the foremost preacher of the devotion to the Sacred Heart in the time of St. Margaret Mary, expressly linked this devotion to the aid of the souls in Purgatory.[6]

Favorite prayers for the poor souls include the *De profundis* (Ps. 129) and various prayers or indulgences that may have salutary effects on the departed (provided the requirements and conditions prescribed by the Church are met). In view of the outstanding power of intercession of Our Lady—we have seen that the Blessed Stanislaus Papczynski taught to especially invoke her as the Immaculate Conception, in fact uniting the devotions to the Sacred Heart, to the Immaculate Heart, and to the souls in Purgatory—the Rosary is the most important prayer after the Mass. What a pity for the poor souls that the traditional habit of praying the Rosary near the coffin of the dead on the day(s) before the funeral has become near extinct!

Furthermore, the litany to the Blessed Virgin, the *Memorare*, and other Marian prayers are also high on the list. The devotion to Our Lady of the Carmel (which implies bearing the scapular), as propagated long ago by St. Simon Stock, offers special graces to the soul of the devotee when it is his turn to go to Purgatory.

In general, it is highly probable that all purely intentioned religious, and even not strictly religious, acts and gestures motivated by love of the deceased are acceptable to God so that they may serve as refreshment for the poor souls: invoking the saints on behalf of them,[7] sprinkling holy water, making the Sign of the Cross with holy water,[8] burning a candle, and so on.

According to an old tradition, one's guardian angel encourages and supports the soul in Purgatory, transmits its prayers, and in the end accompanies it to Heaven. By themselves, the angels cannot mitigate the suffering; not even the saints in Heaven may do this of their own accord, but only if invoked by the living and with God's permission (as it is traditionally assumed). Only the Church Militant can come to the aid of the Suffering Church.

* * *

The suffering souls, in turn, sometimes help the living who help them, either because they pray for their needs,[9] or indirectly, because God rewards the helpers. Maria Anna Lindmayr thought that "God hears the one who prays for them, since the prayer for the least of his brothers is most agreeable to Him."[10] Be this as it may, from a large body of examples over the centuries, it is incontestable that the poor souls are grateful, whether they can effectively pray for their benefactors while in Purgatory or after their entry in heaven. Having enjoined on his hearers the obligation to "assist, to the utmost of our power, these beloved spouses of Jesus Christ [the poor souls], by recommending them every day to God, and by sometimes getting Mass offered for their repose," St. Alphonsus assures that "they certainly will not be ungrateful; they will in return pray for you, and will obtain for you still greater graces, when they shall have entered into the kingdom of God."[11]

St. Catherine of Bologna was one of the great helpers of the poor souls and, for that reason, could testify to the existence of a mutual flow of aid: "They always helped when I had recourse to them."[12]

EPILOGUE

A POOR SOUL APPEARS IN 1870

*T*he following, a rather elaborate and rich case history of the serial apparitions of a soul from Purgatory in 1870, recapitulates a good deal of what we have passed in review.[1]

A monastic in Malines (Belgium), Sister Mary Seraphine, was suddenly seized by a sort of depression, and although she was normally cheerful, now she could not control her mood. She felt oppressed, as though haunted by some invisible shadow that persecuted her wherever she went. Often she felt this invisible presence pulling at her scapular and a "leaden weight" pressed on her right shoulder.[2] She told everything to the Mother Superior and the mistress of novices. Finally, on July 27 she was informed by a letter from France that her father had died on July 17.

From that time, Mary Seraphine often heard sounds of moaning and exclamations similar to those of her father during his illness. Repeatedly, she heard a voice that distinctly implored, "Dear daughter, have mercy on me, have mercy on me, have mercy on me!" On October 4, her pains increased; in addition, she got an excruciating headache.[3] On the evening of October 14, when she was about to fall asleep, she suddenly saw her father standing between the wall and her bed. He looked very sorrowful and was enveloped in flames. She was shocked and called loudly for help. It seemed to her that the flames were scorching her, too.[4]

Next evening, on October 15, and at the same hour, she was kneeling at her bedside and saying the *Salve Regina* before retiring, when she saw her father again, exactly as the first time.

From then on, until his deliverance, she saw him every evening. When he appeared for the second time, she thought her father might have committed some injustice in doing business. But answering her unexpressed thought, he said, "No, I am not guilty of any injustice; I suffer for my continual impatience, and for faults which I cannot mention."[5] She asked if he had not been relieved by the many holy Masses his family had ordered for him. "Oh yes," he replied, "my soul is soothed every morning by a refreshing dew. But that is not sufficient. I am in need of the Stations of the Cross."

When asked what she felt during the apparitions, the sister said, "I feel as if I heard a certain rustling near me, and then I suddenly see my father. His aspect fascinates me, so that I forget where I am. I see and hear only him."

On October 16, he appeared again. The sister had been instructed to say, "All good spirits praise the Lord!" As she received no reaction, she thought it was an evil spirit. But reading her thoughts, her father said, "No, no. I am not a devil!" She replied, "Then say with me: Praise be to Jesus Christ and Mary!" He repeated this ejaculatory prayer twice, then added the words of the Gospel of St. John, "*Et verbum caro factum est.*"[6] He went on, "Alas, alas, I am over six years in purgatory, and you have no compassion with me!"

She replied, "Poor father, how can you speak like this, when it is hardly three months since you died?"[7] He responded, "Oh, you don't know what eternity is! The soul, once having seen God, is consumed with an ardent desire of remaining in His presence."

This fascinating communication harmonizes with the description and analysis of St. Catherine of Genoa and is confirmed by other apparitions. The Dominican priest who appeared to Eugenie von der Leyen described the meeting of the soul with God at particular judgment as "an awful shivering of the soul in adoration (and then sinking down in the Purification)." Near-death experiences suggest the same.

The departed father continues,

> I am sentenced to purgatory for six months; but if your community would pray perseveringly for me, my punishment would be reduced by one half. God has permitted me to implore you continually for my release. How senseless I was to have opposed your vocation. Now I am relieved only in your presence.[8] The rest of my children think I am in heaven, and scarcely one of them now and then says a *De Profundis* for me. Poor Joanna (an old servant) alone continues to pray for me and thereby helps me.

This was really so. His children thought he was in heaven and had written to the sister, "Father died like a saint, and is now in heaven."[9]

"Poor father!" the sister replied. "I am entirely at your service. You may trouble me at will, if only the rest of the community are not disturbed. I will have many prayers said for you. Tell me what you particularly desire."

"I wish that ten Masses be celebrated, and that the Stations of the Cross be visited for me often." His daughter asked if her mother was still in Purgatory. "No; on entering eternity I was informed that she went straight to heaven after her death.[10] You sacrificed your health by nursing her in her last illness, and now I come to trouble you for my deliverance."

On October 17, he appeared again, very sorrowful, but without flames, and complained that he had been less refreshed on the previous day. "Dear father, do you not know that the sisters cannot pray all day? According to our rule we must devote part of our time to our various tasks and labors."

"I do not expect that they pray continually," her father replied, "but they might direct their intentions to my release. Every work, even the least, performed in the state of grace and offered to God, is meritorious and of atoning value, and serves to lessen our punishment."

To offer up daily work, even the most modest activities, for good intentions on earth as well as for the good of the souls, transforming

all occupations into a sacrifice for God—this is the key message of
the 20th-century saint Josemaría Escrivá and his *Opus Dei*. That
way, the distinction between work, prayer, and sacrifice becomes
unimportant.

The man went on:

> If the sisters do not come to my aid, I shall continue to trouble
> you, for the Lord has given me permission.[11] My dear daughter,
> remember the sacrifice you made on the day of your investment;
> now you must bear the consequences. Behold the fiery cistern in
> which I am confined. There are several hundreds of us in it.[12] Oh,
> if people would know what purgatory is! They would suffer every-
> thing in order to escape it and to release the poor souls confined in
> it. You must become a holy religious; you must faithfully observe
> all the rules, even those that may seem to be immaterial. The pur-
> gatory of religious is terrible.[13]

The sister really saw a fiery cistern from which dense clouds of
smoke arose. This vision, she said, "is indelibly inscribed on my
memory." Her father showed her his parched tongue, saying, "I
thirst! I thirst!"[14]

The father returned the following evening. "If I shall have to
remain in purgatory three months more it will seem an eternity,"
he said. "At first I was sentenced to purgatory for many years; and
I owe it to the intercession of the Blessed Virgin that my time was
reduced to a few months." Sister Seraphine told her community
that her father was allowed to ask for her help "in reward for his
good works. Moreover he was devoted to the Blessed Virgin Mary,
in whose honor he received the sacraments on all her feasts.[15] He was
also very charitable; he spared no trouble to assist the unfortunate.
He even begged from door to door to assist in establishing a home
for the Little Sisters of the Poor."

✳   ✳   ✳

Another incident one evening corroborates that the concrete imprints
of hands or fingers, or other miraculous traces of the kind exhibited
in the *Museo del Purgatorio*, are not autonomous actions on the part

of poor souls, but willed by God, and therefore deserve being pondered over seriously and respectfully.

Sister Mary Seraphine offered her father her hand and a copy of the *Imitatio Christi*[16] and asked him to leave the imprint of his hand on her own hand or on the book, because she was haunted by the doubt that these apparitions might be delusions.[17] "No," was the reaction, "I will not do it. The pain you feel is according to the will of God, and your uncertainty is to hasten my deliverance." Later, he nevertheless touched her twice, first on her right shoulder and the next time above her heart, causing intense pain. Strange to say, though no indication appeared on her habit, her skin on both places had a black spot, as she modestly informed her confessor.[18]

By command of her confessor, on October 30, Sister Seraphine asked her father what prayers would be most helpful to be said on All Souls' Day. Instead of answering this question, he complained, "Alas, the world does not believe that the fire of purgatory is similar to that of hell.[19] If a person could but once visit purgatory, he would nevermore commit the least sin, so rigorously are the souls punished." Another time she asked him if he had been released from the cistern, as she had not seen him in it the last three days. "Oh, no, see the proof!" And she saw the cistern, smoke and flames coming from it.[20]

The apparitions received additional objective confirmation when Sister Seraphine's father also appeared to another sister, who was greatly troubled because her own father had died without the Sacraments, after he had neglected his religious duties for a long time. He said to her, "Your father is saved, but he is sentenced to suffer in purgatory for twenty years. For your consolation, however, I am permitted to inform you that your sister N. was released from the flames a short time ago, and is now in heaven." The girl referred to had died 16 years before, when she was only eight years old; and yet she had to suffer so long in Purgatory.[21]

Sister Seraphine also questioned her father about other souls. For example, she asked him one day about the situation of a sister to whom she had been greatly attached. "She is in heaven already for some time," he replied. He was, however, not permitted to say if any sisters of her community were at present in Purgatory. "Do the

souls in purgatory know who prays for them, and are they permitted
to pray for the faithful on earth?" He answered in the affirmative.[22]
He then disclosed that on leaving this world he had seen the infinite majesty of God, the sacred humanity of Jesus Christ, and the
Blessed Virgin Mary and that this vision had left in him a continually increasing and most ardent yearning to see them again.[23] He also
told her that St. Joseph was present at his judgment, that he had
since repeatedly visited Purgatory in company of the Blessed Virgin
to console him, and that he often saw his guardian angel, who came
to comfort him.

✳   ✳   ✳

On November 23, she saw her father as usual; but this time he
seemed closer to her, and her suffering was thereby greatly increased.
She felt as if she were all on fire. He informed her that if the community persevered in prayer as hitherto, he would be released during
the Christmas holidays; also, he was aware of the most secret sufferings offered for the poor souls and immediately[24] felt their beneficial
effect. Directed by her confessor, she asked her father whether it was
true that the torments in Purgatory surpassed in their intensity the
sufferings of the martyrs. "It is but too true," was the reply. And on
whether the members of the Confraternity of Our Lady of Mount
Carmel who wore the scapular are released from Purgatory on the
first Saturday after their death, he said, "Yes, if they have faithfully
fulfilled all the conditions." He also revealed that some souls are
made to stay in Purgatory until the end of the world: "the ones most
tormented[25] and the most forsaken."

On November 30, he told his daughter, "It seems an eternity to
me since I arrived in purgatory. At present my greatest torment is the
intense longing to behold God and to enjoy His possession. I feel
continually elevated towards Him and am at the same time repulsed
and cast into the abyss. Sometimes I am on the edge of the cistern,
seemingly about to be released from it, when I immediately feel the
divine justice detaining me because I have not sufficiently atoned."[26]

She implored her father again, as she had done repeatedly before,
to obtain for her the grace of perseverance amid so many interior and

exterior sufferings. "I have already prayed for you," he said, "and I shall continue to pray for you, my dear daughter. But you will have to suffer still more before I am released."

On December 3, she saw him again. Still sorrowful, he nevertheless appeared greatly relieved. He described to her the intense love of God that he felt and the increasing desire to behold Him. Some time before she had asked him to repeat some of the acts of love that the souls in Purgatory made. He had not complied with her request then,[27] but now he said, "I continually make these three acts of love: O my God, grant me the love with which the Seraphim are inflamed! O my God, grant me still more: grant me the love which inflames the Immaculate Heart of the Blessed Virgin Mary! O my God, why can I not love Thee as Thou lovest Thyself?"

It is clear that this soul was already to a high extent "inflamed" with the love of God, for how else can he find these passionate words of love? He—and the souls in most other apparitions— focuses on their grievous sufferings (among other things) because they come to ask for help; but we can imagine that souls who are so full of love and are ever coming nearer to their Beloved, their definitive, most perfect bliss, must somehow also experience the type of profound joys emphasized by Catherine of Genoa and Francis de Sales.

Next, the man assured his daughter that he implored also for her the love of the Seraphim, adding, "Dear daughter, I am permitted to inform you that, though you are very weak, still you will have to suffer great pain between now and Christmas, on which day I shall be released."[28] She replied, "And then, dear father, what then? Shall I regain my strength, so as to be able to serve God according to our holy rule?"

"That is a mystery not revealed by God," was his response.

From that day until the evening of December 12, the apparitions ceased. Then, and the following evenings, he appeared again, brighter every time. But again, there was a pause from December 14 to 25. Meanwhile, Sister Seraphine suffered so severely that she could hardly visit the chapel. On Christmas night, she succeeded in attending the Midnight Mass, which grace she attributed to the intercession of her father, from whom she expected to receive the announcement of his deliverance. And so it happened. Between the first and the second elevation of the Sacred Host, he appeared to her[29] in supernatural splendor: "My punishment is ended. I come to thank you and your community for all the prayers said for me. From now on I shall pray for you all."

Upon her return to her room, he appeared to her again for the last time to convince her of his release and to thank her again. She implored him to obtain sufficient strength and health to observe the rule. "I will ask for you perfect resignation to the will of God," he told her, "and the grace of entering heaven without having to suffer purgatory."[30] At this last apparition, he was so resplendent that her eyes could scarcely bear the dazzling light. Her joy and happiness were now supreme. She felt an ineffable peace of soul, and she was glad to have the assurance that she had not been the victim of an illusion.

Having thus caught a glimpse of God's glory, her own craving for God was aroused, similar to the yearning of some people with near-death experiences, however more intense and more similar to the interior Purgatory experienced and analyzed by St. Catherine of Genoa, for thereafter, Sister Seraphine was affected by an illness little known to our age: homesickness for Heaven. Her father's yearning desire for the possession of God seemed to have been bequeathed to her. She was somehow consumed; after six months of suffering, borne with a martyr's fortitude, she died at the age of 28. It was Friday, June 23, the octave of the feast of the Sacred Heart, the Source of all mercies the Church and the living faithful can bestow on the mercy-hungry souls of Purgatory.

About the Author

Gerard J. M. van den Aardweg, Ph.D., is a Dutch psychotherapist in private practice. In addition to his work in parapsychology—writing and speaking about near-death experiences and paranormal events such as those detailed in *Hungry Souls*—Dr. van den Aardweg has written extensively on pro-life and pro-family subjects. His previous books include *Education for Life, The Saint of the Ordinary* (about the life of Josemaria Escriva) and *On the Origins and Treatment of Homosexuality*. Dr. van den Aardweg lives in the Netherlands with his wife, with whom he has seven children and seventeen grandchildren.

NOTES

INTRODUCTION

1. Pope John Paul II, General Audience, August 4, 1999. And in the same vein, Pope Benedict XVI has beatifully presented the highlights of the Catholic doctrine on Purgatory in his encyclical *Spe Salvi* (2007).
2. Newman, *Sermons Bearing on Subjects of the Day.*
3. Rev. 21:27.
4. Pope John Paul II, op. cit.
5. Ibid.; emphasis by this author. "Re-proposed," because people's remembrance of much of this is lost.
6. Quote in the brochure of the Arciconfraternità del S. Cuore del Suffragio, Rome, Lungotevere Prati 12.
7. Croiset, *The Devotion to the Sacred Heart of Jesus,* 252.
8. Quoted in Nageleisen, *Charity for the Suffering Souls,* 54.

CHAPTER 1

1. See, for example, Owens, Cook & Stevenson, "Features of 'Near-Death Experience.'" A neurophysiological or neuro-pathological interpretation is very unlikely; the phenomena point to a "transcendental" one (as argued by neurosurgeon Probst, "Nahtod-Erlebnisse").
2. Laun, *So bin ich Gott begegnet,* 7. His youngest son, Andreas, is at present auxiliary bishop of Salzburg, Austria, and a prominent advocate of Catholic moral doctrine.
3. St. Alphonsus says of the reprobate soul: "Though driven back and chased away, she retains her invincible tendency and inclination to a union with God; and her Hell shall consist in seeing herself always drawn to God, and always banished from Him" (Liguori, ed. 1982, 363; sermon 48, 5).

    * Laun's vision of Voltaire recalls the words of St. Paul about "those . . . who obey not the gospel of our Lord Jesus (and) who shall suffer eternal punishment in destruction, from the face of the Lord . . ." (2 Thess. 1:8-9). Concerning the death of Voltaire, Msgr. de Ségur relates (1876, 45): "Everyone knows . . . [that he] expired in a fit of rage and despair. One can still see, in Paris, the room where this tragic scene took place."

4. von der Leyen, *Meine Gespräche mit armen Seelen*, 128–32.

5. The *Letter from Hell* has been published and commented on by a theologian, with authorization by the Diocese of Basel, Switzerland (Krempel, *Brief aus dem Jenseits*).

6. Ibid., 25–27.

7. The story of this soul is consistent with the opinion of St. Alphonsus Liguori: "Alas! The guilty soul that leaves the world in sin, is condemned by herself before the Judge pronounces sentence" (Liguori, 1982, 285). Note that the light shining on the soul and giving it full self-knowledge is in this case a glaring light, not the beautiful, soul-inflaming Light perceived by the soul that is saved.

8. Eccl. 11:3.

9. St. Faustina Kowalska, *Diary: Divine Mercy in My Soul*, 19; nr. 36 (English ed.). Looking at the Christ suffering for our sins, the soul becomes aware of God's love and its own moral misery.

CHAPTER 2

1. Sister Lucia, *Fourth Memoir* (all editions).

2. Sister Lucia, *Como vejo a Mensagem*.

3. Ibid.

4. Holböck, *Die Theologin des Fegfeuers*.

5. According to St. Augustine and St. Thomas, Purgatory is mainly a material fire. St. Augustine remarks that the fact that the immaterial soul feels the pain caused by a material fire in Purgatory is no more wonderful than that the incarnated soul on earth can feel pain that is caused by its material body (*De Civitate Dei*, bk. 21).

6. Quoted in Ursuline nun of Sligo, *Stories of Purgatory and What They Reveal*, 11. Notice that St. Thomas, too, attributes nonmaterial qualities to the fire of Purgatory.

CHAPTER 3

1. With the exception of the very rare cases when God wanted a certain dead to appear for some purpose, like in the story of the witch of Endor (1 Kings or 1 Sam. 28:6-19) or in the life of some saints.

2. Delaporte, *The Devil*, 183–86.

3. The phenomenon of voices who speak at spiritualist sessions may seem unbelievable but has been often testified to by reliable witnesses.

4. Fisher, *Hungry Ghosts*. Fisher wrote his "journey into the realm of darkness and deception" to warn against the trendy channeling practices.
5. Raupert, *Die Geister des Spiritismus*, 73–78. Raupert converted to Catholicism.
6. The famous, erudite Protestant minister Lavater (1741–1801) described several reliable "ghost stories" that apparently concerned souls from Purgatory that begged for holy Masses and pilgrimages. Probably because he could not believe that deceased persons could ask for holy Masses, which he considered Catholic superstition, he argued that they must be demons disguised as human souls. He nonetheless conceded that they had to be a specific type of demons, because if the spiritual aid they had asked was afforded them, they reappeared in lighter, happier forms than before, which otherwise is the normal course of events with apparitions of poor souls. Lavater misinterpreted the nature of these spirits because his belief system forbade him to accept Purgatory, yet he had to admit the authenticity of the stories that came to his attention.
7. For example, during winter of 1945 to 1946, several souls manifested themselves in a house in Silesia (East Poland) where a group of German refugees, some Catholic and some Protestant, hid from the Russian army. One was the spirit of an uncompromisingly Protestant mother who asked her daughter for a holy Mass and apparently "thought it self-evident that the dead live in a place in-between and were allowed to report themselves" (Kudera, Arme Seelen erscheinen in Oberschlesien, 59). Another was the soul of the Protestant sister of one of the refugees, who had died in 1928 and now also came to ask for a holy Mass (January 15, 1946): "'Frieda, please help! One holy Mass, your sister Magdalena.' Nobody can imagine what a terrible feeling it is to know a beloved person in such anguish, besides, an anguish whose extent we do not know. How fervently all of us have prayed for her, one can understand. On the twelfth of February 1946 holy Mass was finally said for her. All of us were in the church and supplicated God to release her. In the evening of this day, at 9.30 . . . came the answer: 'I thank my sweet sister Elfriede (Frieda) for the holy Mass and I am already delivered'" (ibid., 70).

   Another example: Among the affidavits taken from the many witnesses of the manifestations of the soul of Johann Klement Zwespenbauer during 1641 and 1642 in Pressburg (or Pozsony, the present Bratislava), several came from Protestants. (The authentic reports of the case have been studied and described by Alexander Gaibl, Abbot in Pressburg/Poszony, 1910.)
8. Blumhardt, *Die Krankheitsgeschichte des Gottliebin Dittus*, 36–38. For the sake of clarity, we omit the role of the pious Gottliebin, to whom the spirits came.

CHAPTER 4

1. Quoted in Klimsch, *De dooden leven*, 199.
2. Luke 16:31

3. de Ségur, *L'Enfer*, 34–40. Several books of Msgr. de Ségur received papal recommendations.
4. Voltaire was the prototype and role model of the unbelieving freethinkers of that time and, in a certain sense, of the modern post-Christian secular humanist as well.
5. In one of his nightly visions, Don Bosco was obliged to press his hand against the outer wall of Hell. It not only caused him intense pain, but the next morning his hand was swollen "and the skin of my palm peeled off" (*Brown, Dreams, Visions & Prophecies of Don Bosco*, 227).

CHAPTER 5

1. Apparitions of the dead are reported in most, if not all, pagan cultures before Christianity. In the light of the fact that some poor souls in recent apparitions manifest animal features, to express the vices they must atone for (von der Leyen, op. cit.), one may wonder if such apparitions didn't occur in ancient times as well, giving rise to the confused idea that some souls come back (reincarnate) in animals.
2. A wealth of ethnological evidence for this view has been amassed by the Viennese scientist Father Wilhelm Schmidt, *Der Ursprung der Gottesidee*.
3. Quoted by Nageleisen, op. cit., 16
4. In the Christian mystical tradition, Purgatory is sometimes represented as a lake as well, and not always as a lake of fire.
5. 2 Mach. 12:43, 46.
6. Around 160 BC.
7. Personal communication to this author by American Rabbi Leonard Levy; May 31, 2007.
8. I am grateful to Rabbi Leonard Levy for sending me the complete English text of this prayer. That this prayer is alive in the Jewish tradition is confirmed by incidents such as the religious commemoration by the New York Jews in November 1905 of their murdered brothers during a Russian pogrom. Over and again they "cried from their hearts" the first three words, "El, Malei Rachamim," as an ejaculatory prayer, imploring God's mercy for the dead (Meagher, *How Christ Said the First Mass*, 276).
9. The one-year limit of the Jewish notion of Purgatory could be a later addition. However, the period of a year is thought of some significance in Catholic tradition, too; a special holy Mass for the deceased is often said on the date of their death.
10. Quoted in Nageleisen, op. cit., 25.
11. Holböck, *Fegfeuer*, 35–36. Holböck has authored several wonderful and singularly informative books on theological subjects. He was a professor of theology at the University of Salzburg, Austria. He died in 2002. According to Holböck, the authenticity of the *Acta* of St. Perpetua is historically beyond doubt.

CHAPTER 6

1. Quoted in Nageleisen, op. cit., 23.
2. Sermon 34 (*De verbis Apostolorum*), quoted in Schouppe, *Purgatory Explained*, 150.
3. St. Augustine, *De cura pro mortuis gerenda ad Paulinum*, written about 421.
4. Quoted in Schouppe, op. cit., 246.
5. Nageleisen, op. cit., 188.
6. Ibid., 68.
7. Professor Holböck (*Fegfeuer*) gives a long list of saintly "friends and helpers" of the souls in Purgatory from early Christian times onward and relates their efforts for these souls, who often visited them.
8. Nageleisen, op. cit., 168 and 112, respectively.
9. Blessed Father Claude de la Colombière (a Jesuit), after convincing himself of the genuineness of the Lord's communications to Margaret Mary, became the prominent preacher of the devotion to the Sacred Heart. In a prayer of offering all of one's religious acts, virtues, and merits to the Heart of Jesus, he explicitly asked Christ to distribute them to the souls in Purgatory (Croiset, op. cit., 63).
10. Nageleisen, op. cit., 111. Underlined by the author. Indirectly, the saints in Heaven may help, upon our prayers.
11. Holböck, *Die Theologin des Fegfeuers*, 137. Many recent as well as older cases of apparitions of poor souls contain verifiable elements that could and have been examined.
12. This is not so unlikely when one realizes that, in the last analysis, it is not the corporal human brain but the immaterial human consciousness that perceives pain.
13. St. Faustina Kowalska, op. cit., 11, nr. 20.
14. Quoted in Nageleisen, op. cit., 112.
15. Canon XXX, Session VI; and Session XXV.
16. Nr 1030, 1472.

CHAPTER 7

1. This and the following quotes from Catherine of Genoa's so-called *Tract on Purgatory* are taken from her *Purgation and Purgatory*, 71–87.
2. Our notions and words are necessarily borrowed from the material world of space and time in which we live. Yet our immaterial soul can grasp, through these very words and images, at least a glimmer of the afterlife. This is true for all accounts of mystical experiences and also for near-death experiences.
3. Holböck, *Die Theologin des Fegfeuers*.
4. Ibid., 101–2. In fact, St. Cathcrine did not write this *Tract* herself, but her communications were most probably written down by her confessor Marabotto.

5. Compare this expression to the later formulation of the Council of Trent concerning "the debt of temporal punishment to be discharged" (Canon XXX, Session VI).
6. We may note how the near-death experience of Hellmut Laun harmonizes with the analysis of St. Catherine (the latter being more profound and penetrating, of course). Laun actually experienced a small portion of what St. Catherine describes.
7. Nageleisen, op. cit., 49.
8. Kaplan, *The Aryeh Kaplan Reader*, 179–80.
9. Nageleisen, op. cit., 53.
10. Klimsch, op. cit., 182.
11. Holböck, *Die Theologin des Fegfeuers*, 101.
12. Holböck, *Fegfeuer*, 95.
13. See note 2.
14. de Sales, *Treatise on the Love of God*, 92–93.
  * The remarks of Pope Benedict XVI on Purgatory in his encyclical *Spe Salvi* (of November 2007), in particular nr. 47, reflect the same view as proposed in this chapter.

CHAPTER 8

1. We borrow these data from the brochure of the Arciconfraternità, Rome, no date.
2. See next chapter.
3. The brochure of the "Museo" references to the bulletin *Il Purgatorio visitato dalla carità dei fedeli* of the Arch-fraternity of the Sacred Heart of the Suffrage (published since 1894). See the brochure for more detailed documentation of the pieces.
4. "Spook" phenomena often precede apparitions of deceased, possibly to prepare the seer.
5. This reminds us of St. Bridget's remark that the souls in Purgatory pray for the well-being of the souls of their beloved on earth.
6. Date of death not mentioned.
7. German text of the page of the prayer book: "*so tilge in jenem Leben aus . . . (Barm)herzigkeit die Folgen ihrer Fehlschritte, und ruf sie zur Krone der . . . Unsterblichkeit . . . der vollendeten Tugend im himmlischen Reiche . . .*" and "*(gewähre?) den Seelen der Verstorbenen die (ewige) Ruhe . . .*" and "*(Gewähre) ihnen die ewige Ruhe, und das ewige Licht (erleuchte) ihnen. . . .*"
8. Carty, *Padre Pio the Stigmatist*, 259, 248, respectively.
9. Jouët, *Un petit tour par le purgatoire*.

CHAPTER 9

1. One may wonder if apparitions who only left an imprint of their left hand have been left-handed persons in life?

2. That is a matter of prudence. The relic would easily become a distracting tourist attraction in a place where all attention must go to the Marian shrine. The *Museo del Purgatorio* in Rome is a different thing. There, not an isolated item but a collection (with explanations) within a church that is wholly dedicated to the aid of the souls in Purgatory invites the serious and respectful faithful rather than the uninstructed or ignorant tourist who does not know what to make of it or who would react disrespectfully.

3. In the former Palace of the Kings outside Warsaw, now a museum, one can see nearly identical boxes with photos of important personalities from that time.

4. The then-prior of the monastery, Father Jerzy Tomzinski, wrote in 1975 that, indeed, the *corporale* was still preserved in his monastery, "alas without any written report whatsoever." The accompanying story was merely "an oral tradition" (Siegmund, "Das Fortleben," 480–81; Siegmund, "Das Phänomen"). Nevertheless, it is difficult to assume that no testimonial document has existed because it would be strange that when such an extraordinary relic had been wrapped up that carefully, it was neglected to ensure the correct transmission of the facts connected to it to posterity. One hopes that a document will turn up some day either in the archives of the monastery or someplace else.

5. Published in Keller, *Hundertfünfundsechzig Armenseelen-Geschichten*, 274–75.

6. The letter of Father Tomzinski to Professor Siegmund does not mention the doubt of the priest about survival after the death when he folded the *corporale* up, and instead of confirming that the other priest was "long dead," it states that the fiery hand was impressed "shortly after his death." These differences indicate that the "oral tradition" had lost some interesting details between about 1880 to 1890, when Father Reichel wrote his report, and 1975. We believe that the version of Father Reichel is the most dependable.

7. There are more examples of apparitions who read the thoughts of persons to whom they appear.

8. This type of agreement among friends seems to have been more frequent in the 19th century, whether seriously meant (see the agreement between Count Orloff and his friend the general, chap. 4).

9. The then-24-year-old Don Bosco did not have to wait so long. Three days after Comollo's death (in 1839), Giovanni Bosco and the about 20 other seminarians in the same dormitory woke up by a thundering noise, as if a carriage with enormous horses rushed toward them, and everything around

was shaking. All of a sudden, the door of the dormitory opened and the noise entered the room. Then it ceased abruptly, and in a sepulchral silence, accompanied by a glaring light, the voice of Comollo exclaimed three times, "Bosco, I am saved!" The noise set in again, even louder now, as if a hurricane had hit the house, and then moved away. In this case, no visible trace of the message from eternity is left, but a group of fellow seminarians could testify to its veracity (Auffray, *Dom Bosco*, chap. 2).

CHAPTER 10

1. As one of their functions is obviously to substantiate requests for holy Masses and other suffrages, it is not surprising that they are primarily encountered where and when belief in Purgatory and the custom to pray for the souls is alive.

2. Proceedings of the investigation are in possession of the diocesan Curia, Foligno. Msgr. Klimsch, who has described the case, saw the imprint himself. In his book, he mentions other cases of burned-in hands in Germany: for example, a hand mark in a blue cotton handkerchief in Orlach (Württemberg), and one in a missal of Mrs. Schmidt-Walker in Kreuzfeld (Nassau), which would still be preserved in the parish archive in the 1930s (Klimsch, op. cit., 146, 166, 174, respectively).

3. Abbot Dom Gaibl critically reexamined the old documents in 1910, to save the case from oblivion. At least one of the relics did still exist in his time.

4. Grabinski, an experienced student of cases of burned-in hands, could photograph this handkerchief in 1917 (pictured in Grabinski, *Spuk oder Geistererscheinungen*, 80).

5. Grabinski described the case and published the photograph of the hand mark he made in 1918 (Grabinski, op. cit., 79–85, 95). On the pieces of cloth from both Pflochsbach and Fuchsmühl, Grabinski noticed a fiery-yellow tone, suggesting scorching heat.

6. Ibid., 90–103. Photographs: Grabinski, op. cit., 112; Siegmund, 1982, 420.

7. This reminds us of the loud blow accompanying the imprinting of the hand at Fuchsmühl.

8. Grabinski, op. cit., 106, 133.

9. Ibid., 107–13. In 1918, Grabinski could interview two trustworthy witnesses—a priest and a scholar—who had watched the event from close by and who also saw the hand imprint in the prayer book, which had penetrated many pages.

10. The Latin text (of the Tridentine Mass that was in use at that time): "*Propitiare, quaesumus Domine, animae famuli tui N. pro qua hostiam laudis tibi immolamus, majestatem tuam suppliciter deprecantes: ut per haec piae placationis officia, pervenire mereatur ad requiem sempiternam. . . .*" Note

the striking similarity between this splendid Catholic prayer and the traditional Jewish prayer for the defunct *El, Malei Rachamim* (chap. 5).

11. After World War II, Grabinski checked the details of the story with the priests who had firsthand information of it and examined the altar missal, which was no longer in the possession of the church but of one of these priests. For privacy reasons, he did not mention the name of the town or the parish. Also, Professor Bender, the well-known German professor of parapsychology, examined the missal and declared the origin of the burns inexplicable by natural causes (Grabinski, op. cit., 141–49).

12. Siegmund, 1981 a., 422, shows the photograph of a burned-in hand in a prayer book that exactly covers a prayer for the dead.

CHAPTER 11

1. Apparition of 1916, described by Sister Lucia (de Marchi, 1985 ed., 46).
2. Klimsch, op. cit., 229.
3. von der Leyen, op. cit., 119.
4. di Rocca, *Mutter Anna Maria Lindmayr O.C.D.*, 33.
5. Cf. the case of the "dead man" who appeared to Padre Pio (chap. 16).
6. di Rocca, op. cit., 30. Some souls appear first in their previous earthly figure and show their inner condition later on; some first appear in symbolic shapes and develop to normal forms in proportion as their expiation process proceeds (sped up by the help of the living).
7. von der Leyen, op. cit., 94.
8. di Rocca, op. cit., 31.
9. Look at the dehumanized figures of several poor souls who came to Eugenie von der Leyen. An exceptionally stark example was the soul that manifested itself as a snake. In later apparitions, it gradually developed human features and turned out to be the soul of a nun whose outward religious life had been a big lie. On February 25, 1926, Eugenie noted in her diary, "I have looked at it carefully. It is dark grey with white stripes. It is altogether impossible that it would not be a graspable body, that it is only a product of the fantasy. . . . I have pushed the snake somewhat with my stick, then it unrolled directly. It was terrible, but I wanted to see, to report it" (von der Leyen, op. cit., 144). This is not an apparition from the age of the Baroque but from the 20th century.

   * The question may arise whether the (false) ancient Indian notion of the reincarnation of some souls into the body of animals may originally have come from similar, erroneously interpreted apparitions.

10. Souls from Purgatory ask for prayers and sacrifices, for works of mercy, wherefore it is understandable that they principally go to Catholics; on the whole, Protestantism had abolished these practices. The primary reason of the souls' coming to Catholics is, of course, their need for

holy Masses, to profit from the Sacrifice of Christ's expiating Body and Blood. Therefore, also deceased Protestants sometimes appear to Catholics to ask for holy Masses. Maria Anna Lindmayr is an example: "Altogether, many of those who have lived and are died in Lutherdom . . . [because they erred out of ignorance] received from God the grace of repentance at the end of their life. . . . They said to me: I should and could help them; because, since they had not lived in the true Church, they were also cut off from all means of help and took refuge to me. Those souls demanded very particularly the holy Sacrifice of the Mass and holy Communion [offered up for them]" (di Rocca, op. cit., 32).

11. Ibid., 35.

12. von der Leyen, op. cit., 52, 125, 150. On a certain occasion, she asked the soul of a nun who had died five years before in a French monastery why she appeared to her (in Germany) and not to the sisters of her own community. "I am there oftentimes, but they don't see me." "Why do I see you and the almost saintly women there do not?" ". . . You can detach yourself." "Detach from what?" "From yourself"(147). So souls from Purgatory are probably more often near the living than the latter could imagine; however, they cannot make themselves known and ask what they want. The same is affirmed by other visionaries.

13. "I noticed the poor souls already at the age of twelve," wrote Mother Lindmayr (di Rocca, op. cit., 29).

14. For example, of 43 cases described by Holböck (*Fegfeuer*), 27 (60 percent) are women.

CHAPTER 12

1. Rogalewski, Lumen Marianorum, 219.

2. For example, "a Divine vision which was imprinted in my soul with respect to founding a Congregation of the Immaculate Conception of the Blessed Virgin Mary" (Ibid., 193 et seq.).

3. Ibid., 222 (emphasis by this author). A profession shortly before his death, in 1701, says, "I, Stanislaus of Jesus and Mary, as Superior of the Polish Order of the Immaculate Conception of the Blessed Virgin Mary, whose *goal is to help the deceased and pastors . . .*" (303, emphasis by this author).

4. Ibid., 305.

5. Ibid., 211, 219.

6. The same Polish king who, a couple of years later (in 1683), would turn the battle near Vienna against the Turks into a victory for the Christian (Catholic) armies and save the European continent from the Islam (curiously, on a date that in our days got such a negative ring: September 11).

7. Rogalewski, op. cit., 219.

8. Ibid.

9. Ibid., 220–21.

CHAPTER 13

1. St. Augustine warned that it would be "reckless" to deny the apparitions of the dead (Nageleisen, op. cit., 72).
2. von der Leyen, op. cit., 49–54.
3. The apparition is also perceived by the sense of touch: the presence is something material.
4. From other apparitions of Eugenie von der Leyen and others, it may be gathered that the more impure the soul, the more inhuman and deformed its appearance. Some souls do not or cannot speak before reaching some minimal stage of purification, and when they speak, it is usually telegram-style, their answers being no more than a few key words that are all the more emotional and impressive.
5. A perfectly normal reaction!
6. Sprinkling holy water for the poor souls: an old, but efficient gesture of charity.
7. Being unsympathetic: this means that the old personality traits (habits) still stick to the soul in Purgatory; this we would perhaps not expect. Also the man's aggressiveness was still alive.
8. "Repentance" as a condition to be saved: a truth often skipped over in the "optimistic" belief that everyone, irrespective of the way he lives, goes to Heaven.
9. Souls in Purgatory cannot pray for themselves, but they seem intent on accompanying the praying of the living.
10. Same experience as Mother Maria Anna Lindmayr two centuries earlier (chap. 11).
11. As a result of Eugenie's suffrage, no doubt. As soon as Fritz needs less help, it seems time for another soul to usurp her strength!
12. Evidently, his aggressiveness was burning away.
13. This is to remind us that all apparitions are directed by God.
14. In the process of helping the poor soul, a bond of affection may grow, as in earthly life.
15. von der Leyen, op. cit., 69–84.
16. Probably in order to sweetly urge Eugenie to pray for her.
17. Even aversion to the religious—a habit of thinking and feeling—thus seems part of the soul's "rust of sin" as long as it is not burned away. Who would have imagined that?
18. Wildness, hostility, and so on: these behaviors impress as obsessive, compulsive, automatic, as if these drives continue working in the soul the same way as they were in life. Another very aggressive soul, who behaved "like a mad dog," declared to Eugenie, "The evil is still in me. It still sticks to me" (op. cit., 131, 134). We might perhaps suppose that these "evil impulses" torment the soul in Purgatory as they may torment the psyche of the living. In the living, we would diagnose them

as neurotic, masochistic, self-destructive, or even as psychopathic. Such conditions then seem to be prolonged in afterlife. A wild, aggressive, desperate person suffers from these emotions and has no peace. Restless souls, impure souls, they must yearn for peace. Hence, *Requiescant in pace* (May they rest in peace).

19. The "wild" soul is divided in two parts; if it had no other side, it would not be in Purgatory but in Hell.

20. Thus furious ghosts are not always demons, although one can imagine they are (initially) misidentified as such.

21. A demon would behave the same way, and yet this is a poor soul.

22. Op. cit., 132, 87, 107, 123, respectively.

23. The ability to speak as a measure for the soul's progress; see note 4.

24. Nevertheless, her sacrifice out of love for old Heinz must have benefited him.

25. Eugenie exemplifies that it is self-denying love that atones for the dead. The smallness of the gesture becomes great by the unselfish love that motivates it. Immediately, a transformation is effected in this suffering soul. The story of St. Francis's overcoming his repulsion and kissing the leper comes to mind.

26. Father Wieser makes an interesting observation that is important for the psychology of people with compulsive inclinations to evil deeds, aggression, revenge, and self-destructive behaviors in various forms, the type of persons often evaluated as "less accountable." It may well be that demonic influences play a role in many cases of compulsive and obsessive needs and drives (which need not be precisely possessions proper, but rather partial possessions, or demonic obsessions and oppressions).

27. "In torment" is also the mind on earth who discharges his frustrations in destructive deeds or crimes.

28. Significantly, the burn marks on some prayer books are placed on prayers to the holy Virgin, such as the fingerprints on the prayer book of Mr. Schitz (chap. 8) and the hand on the photograph in the article of Siegmund, 1982, 422.

29. Grave sin may usher the devil in the soul.

CHAPTER 14

1. St. Faustina Kowalska, op. cit., nr. 20.
2. Ibid.
3. The morning with its sobering effect . . .

CHAPTER 15

1. The cases described in this book are virtually all from Western Europe. It is very likely that they can be found all over the world, in Ireland, North and South America, Russia, and in developing countries. If there are no examples known in certain parts of the world, that might simply be because they are not registered or reported on and so easily fall into oblivion.
2. Holböck, *Fegfeuer*, 144–47; Ernst, *Die Seherin aus dem Ruhrgebiet*. Pope Pius X was acquainted with her; he has sent her a small present and a letter.
3. A singularly balanced personality, without any indication of neurotic or hysteric emotionality. Quoted in Ernst, op. cit., 18–23.
4. Ibid., 66.
5. Ibid., 85.
6. Chap. 2.
7. Ernst, op. cit., 81–82.
8. Ibid., 87.
9. Ibid., 82.
10. Ibid., 68.
11. Ibid., 85.
12. Chap. 13; July 6.
13. Ernst, op. cit., 86.

CHAPTER 16

1. Schug, *A Padre Pio Profile*, 77.
2. "Now who will think of the holy souls?" It is a bitter fact that since so many pious customs for the defunct were practically abolished in the Catholic Church in the wake of the Second Vatican Council, the devotion to the poor souls has dramatically decreased. In other words, a precious work of charity has been terribly damaged.
3. Schug, op. cit., 101–4.
4. Padre Pio obviously tried to conceal the whole supernatural event. Yet he may well have told the truth when he affirmed that the door was open. One possible explanation could be that his own or his visitor's guardian angel intervened. Like "an angel of the Lord" caused the "iron gate" of St. Peter's prison to "open of its own accord" (Acts 12:7-10).

CHAPTER 17

1. Wagner, *Das grosse Wagnis*, 126–38.
2. The first stage of many visual apparitions.
3. The powerful intercession of the Blessed Virgin is often asked by the poor souls.
4. Poor souls mostly do not speak on their own initiative.

5. Poor souls are often allowed to ask for the aid of their living family members in the first place. In the case of Ruth, first comes her husband, her closest family member, then her grandmother. That is in accord with a very natural principle, and it contains the practical lesson for all the living with departed family members that it is their special duty to pray for them. Family bonds of love and of responsibility reach over the grave.

6. St. Catherine of Genoa taught that in proportion as the rust of sin disappears, the soul becomes more loving, because it can receive or contain more of God's love (chap. 7). We can notice this in all serial apparitions where the soul receives help from the living.

7. Do we ever see that spiritualist mediums or other occult "seers" of the dead sacrifice themselves so selflessly and lovingly? Rather, we see the opposite.

8. Slugs: "the rust of sin," sinful habits or tendencies that are the effects of sins on the soul (chap. 7).

9. Not exceptionally, the soul that is helped immensely by the suffrages has nevertheless not yet arrived at its final destiny. In these cases, it must be concluded that God judged that the limits of compassion/mercy had been reached and that the soul has to expiate the remaining part of its debt on its own.

10. Guardian angels who, of course, execute the Will of God.

11. This note of Ruth's on the presence of poor souls around the locations where they lived reminds us of the not infrequent "idea" or "feeling" of relatives that a departed person has been near them, in one way or another. An Amsterdam clinical psychologist found in a follow-up study of a few years that of 300 persons whose marriage partner had died, between 20 and 25 percent said they sometimes felt the deceased near them or even saw him or her (Schut, "Results of a Study").

12. They urge her to seek the help of the parish priest (Father Wagner).

CHAPTER 18

1. St. Augustine, *Confessions*, bk. 9, XI, 27.

2. Remember that Padre Pio told holy souls with astounding confidence that he would "offer a Mass" for them "and you will be liberated."

3. St. Francis de Sales relates the apparition of a murdered son to his mother to inform her that his whole period of expiation, which should have lasted for years, was remitted because she had heroically forgiven his murderer and even had hid him to protect him from being arrested (quoted in Nageleisen, op. cit., 153).

4. The practice of offering daily work for the poor souls is not so well-known, although it is a logical consequence of the Christian sanctification of ordinary work (St. Josemaría Escrivá, *Homélies*). Some poor souls expressly asked for this form of expiation; for example, a soul who appeared to Ursula Hibbeln (Ernst, op. cit., 71) and the soul whose

story is reproduced in the epilogue. Otherwise, an element of sacrifice or mortification is always inherent in doing one's ordinary work in a way that is pleasing to God, which enhances the value of this form of suffrage for the suffering souls.

5. Prévot, *Love, Peace, and Joy*, 38.
6. Croiset, op. cit., 63.
7. Nageleisen, op. cit., 109.
8. Ibid., 132.
9. "Gregory of Valencia maintains that the souls in Purgatory pray for the faithful in general, but particularly for those who were very dear to them on earth. Bellarmine, Suarez, Sylvius, Gotti, Jungmann and many others are of the same opinion" (Nageleisen, op. cit., 278).
10. di Rocca, op. cit., 26.
11. St. Alphonsus, *Sermons for All the Sundays of the Year*, Sermon 30, nr. 12.
12. Nageleisen, op. cit., 299.

EPILOGUE

1. First published in 1872, with ecclesiastical approbation, it has been relayed by Nageleisen, op. cit., also as the last chapter of his outstanding book on Purgatory (343–53). The story has been well examined. We reproduce here the relation of Nageleisen, however, slightly abbreviated.
2. This gesture of the "shadow" that evidently claimed her attention is meaningful. It seems as if the ghost wanted to incite her to pray for the intercession of Our Lady (the devotion promoted by St. Simon Stock). The significance of the pressure on her right shoulder is not clear; is it symbolic of her having to carry a cross for her deceased father? Also Maria Anna Lindmayr wrote that the poor souls used to pull at her habit (di Rocca, op. cit., 29).
3. Her well-endured sufferings must have been substitute penance for her father.
4. Probably a real sense experience.
5. The soul reads or knows her thoughts—at least certain thoughts. This seems to occur often; its meaning is, however, unsure. He had already pointed to his impatience as the sin he had to do penance for by his moaning and exclamations, his typical reactions during his illness. Impatience is regularly mentioned as a reason for purification in the afterlife (see the story of the pious Sister Mary of St. Luigi Gonzaga, chap. 8; or the impatient husband of Ruth in chap. 17). Impatience with suffering is an imperfection, because the human will does not conform to the divine Will.
6. "And the Word was made flesh." The father points to Christ's Redemption, which enables the souls to be purified in Purgatory. The soul in Purgatory praises and adores the Incarnated God who saved him and is merciful to him.

7. The intensity of suffering in Purgatory seems to prolong the sense of time; a short time on earth is experienced as an eternity in Purgatory.

8. God's Providence must have foreseen and willed her future aid to her father when calling her to the religious life. This may illuminate the many purposes and facets of God's actions of mercy with respect to every individual person. His providential actions in the life of one person may involve and extend to family members.

9. Neglect of the poor souls is rampant in present-day Catholicism. At funerals, it is a stereotype remark that the deceased "is now with God," or "in heaven," and other possibilities are not even considered. The humble Ruth passed on the same complaint from souls who were forgotten and forsaken by their family.

10. If such "happy endings" probably occur only in the minority of cases, it is fortunate that they are nonetheless regularly mentioned by souls from Purgatory.

11. God's permission and not the initiative of the soul must be seen behind all manifestations from Purgatory.

12. Cisterns, pits, and so on—this is how the soul experiences Purgatory. The image of the cistern is a traditional one. For example, the Dutch St. Lydwine of Schiedam (1380–1433), who visited Purgatory like the Blessed Stanislaus Papczynski 300 years later, and the 20th-century St. Faustina Kowalska saw the suffering souls imprisoned in cisterns (Meuffels, *De heilige Liduina van Schiedam*). Maybe this is to be interpreted as the experience of being imprisoned in one's "rust of sin."

13. For *noblesse oblige*, more grace means more responsibility. The burn traces of apparitions of religious and priests illuminate this statement of the father; in contrast, they seem privileged as it comes to being permitted to appear in order to ask for suffrage.

14. Both the pain of loss (of God) and the pain of the senses seem expressed by his thirst.

15. The devotion to Our Lady is a great asset to the Catholic, both in this life and the next.

16. Reminds of the burned-in fingers (1815) in the copy of the *Imitatio* in the *Museo del Purgatorio* (chap. 8). Was Sister Mary Seraphine familiar with such events that she asked for the same proof?

17. Some external confirmation for the authenticity of the apparitions came from the following incident: when another sister got a terrible toothache, Sister Seraphine proposed her to pray for her father and ask relief of her pain in return. No sooner had this sister done so than the pain vanished.

18. In the case of Mother Isabella (chap. 8), the touch first burned a hole in her tunic and then in her chemise. But a burn spot on the body without traces of burning on the clothes is less incredible if we compare it with the extraordinary, medically inexplicable, but well-established phenomena known as "spontaneous combustion": some people

have reportedly died after their body was suddenly ablaze with some mysterious, intense fire that left it charred within a very short time; even more stunning, however, is that their clothes were entirely intact and did not show marks of scorching (Michell and Richard, *Phenomena*; this phenomenon reeks of the occult, but there is no link with Purgatory).

19. In line with the Catholic tradition (St. Thomas) and the orthodox Jewish notion of *gehinnom*.

20. A reminder that a poor soul who appears as a normal living person may show only a part of his reality.

21. The perplexed reader may suppose—wish—that the expiatory afflictions of this girl were relatively mild; yet the suffering of young children in Purgatory is well documented. Recall the vision of St. Perpetua of her seven-year-old brother, Dinocrates, in the early third century (chap. 5). Admitting that also little children can commit faults for which they bear full responsibility, the idea of a young child in Purgatory is nonetheless difficult to understand, possibly because we can scarcely imagine the extent of evil in even the least sin.

22. This is also the opinion of many authors, among them several saints. It seems logical.

23. He repeats what he has said before about what happens right after death and adds beautiful new information.

24. The poor souls profit *immediately* from every assistance by the living, be it ever so little; this signals God's eagerness to relieve and release them.

25. To the end of the world: If Our Lady had not given the example of Amélia and thereby confirmed the ancient tradition, we would perhaps not believe this. That these souls are the "most tormented" need probably not be taken literally; it could mean that some or even many of these souls belong to the category with the heaviest quantity of "rust of sin" at death, but it could also be a manner of saying that they are the most pitiful because of the seemingly endless duration of their frustrated longing for God. This amendment is suggested by the "theory" of Sister Lucia in her attempt to account for Amélia's fate (chap. 2).

26. Being torn apart between the upward-"gravitating" force of the yearning for God and the withholding impurities that still stick to the soul. St. Catherine of Genoa said just that.

27. Why not? No doubt, there was a spiritual reason. Nothing is said or done by these souls for superficial motives.

28. On the day the "Word was made flesh," (*Verbum caro factum est*).

29. One easily finds more examples of the final, glorious apparition of a soul at this august moment, to announce its entry in Heaven.

30. Her heroic suffering for her father, we can assume, has earned her this reward. Minimally, those who helped the poor souls seem to receive extra help when in Purgatory themselves.

BIBLIOGRAPHY

Auffray, A., S.D.B. *Dom Bosco* (Portuguese Edition of the original French). S. Paulo: Editorial Dom Bosco, 1969.

Blumhardt, J.C. *Die Krankheitsgeschichte des Gottliebin Dittus (The illness history of Gottliebin Dittus)*. Hamburg: L. Appel Verlag, 1950 (Orig. pub. 1844).

Brown, E.M. *Dreams, Visions & Prophecies of Don Bosco*. New Rochelle, NY: Don Bosco Publications, 1986.

Carty, Ch.M. *Padre Pio the Stigmatist*. Rockford, IL: TAN Books, 1973.

St. Catherine of Genoa. *Purgation and Purgatory*. London: SPCK, 1979.

Croiset, J., S.J. *The Devotion to the Sacred Heart of Jesus*. Rockford, IL: TAN Books, 1988 (Orig. pub. 1691).

Delaporte. *The Devil: Does He Exist? And What Does He Do?* Rockford, IL: TAN Books, 1982 (Orig. French ed. 1871).

Ernst, R. *Die Seherin aus dem Ruhrgebiet (The seer from the Ruhrgebiet)*. Stein am Rhein, Switzerland: Christiana Verlag, 1988.

Escrivá de Balaguer, St. Josemaría. *Homélies: Amis de Dieu (Sermons: Friends of God)*. Paris: Fayard/Mame, 1981.

Kowalska, St. (Maria) Faustina. *Diary: Divine Mercy in My Soul*. Stockbridge MA: Marians of the Immaculate Conception, 2001.

Fisher, J. *Hungry Ghosts: An Investigation into Channeling and the Spirit World*. London: Grafton Books, 1990.

Gaibl, Abbot A.M. *Narratio rei admirabilis oder Beschreibung einer wunderlichen That (Description of a miraculous event)*. Pressbug/Poszony, Bratislava: Aktiengesellschaft, 1910.

Grabinski, B. *Spuk oder Geistererscheinungen: Oder was sonst? (Spook or apparitions of spirits: Or what else?)*, vol. 2. Gröbenzell, Germany: S. Hacker, 1970.

Holböck, F. *Fegfeuer: Leiden, Freuden und Freunde der Armen Seelen (Purgatory: Suffering, joys and friends of the poor souls)*. Stein am Rhein, Switzerland: Christiana Verlag, 1980.

Holböck, F. *Die Theologin des Fegfeuers: Hl. Catharina von Genua (The Theologian of Purgatory: St. Catherine of Genoa)*. Stein am Rhein, Switzerland: Christiana Verlag, 1980.

John Paul II (pope). *General Audience*. Wednesday, August 4, 1999.

Jouët, Father V. *Un petit tour par le purgatoire (A small tour through purgatory)*. 2nd ed. Sherbrooke, Québec: Éditions St-Raphaël, 1933.

Kaplan, Rabbi A. *The Aryeh Kaplan Reader*. Brooklyn, NY: Mesorah Publications, 1985.

Keller, J.A. *Hundertfünfundsechzig Armenseelen-Geschichten (One hundred and sixty stories of poor souls)*. Mainz: F. Kirchheim, 1891.

Klimsch, Msgr. R. *De dooden leven (The dead are alive)*. The Hague: Pax, 1940 (Dutch ed. of the German orig.).

Krempel, B., C.P. *Brief aus dem Jenseits (Letter from the other side)*. Basel, Switzerland: Verlag Nazareth, 1942.

Kudera, E. *Arme Seelen erscheinen in Oberschlesien, 1945-1946: Ein Tatsachenbericht (Poor souls appear in Upper Silesia: A report of the facts)*. Gröbenzell, Deutschland: S. Hacker, 1975.

Laun, H. *So bin ich Gott begegnet (That way I encountered God)*. Eichstätt, Deutschland: Franz-Sales-Verlag, 1996.

Lavater, J.C. *Von Gespensten und Nachtgeistern (On phantoms and spirits of the night)*. Zürich, Switzerland, orig. 1670.

von der Leyen, E. *Meine Gespräche mit armen Seelen (My conversations with poor souls)*. Stein am Rhein, Switzerland: Christiana Verlag, 1980.

Liguori, St. Alphonsus. *Sermons for All the Sundays of the Year*. Rockford, IL: TAN Books, 1982.

Lucia, Sister Maria. *Fourth Memoir*.

Lucia, Sister Maria. *Como vejo a Mensagem através dos tempos e dos acontecimenos (How I see the Message in the course of the time and after all that happened)*. Fátima (P): Secretariado dos Pastorinhos, 2006.

Meagher, J.L. *How Christ Said the First Mass*. Rockford, IL: TAN Books, 1984 (Orig. pub. 1906).

Meuffels, H., C.M. *De heilige Liduina van Schiedam (St. Lydwine of Schiedam)*. Den Bosch, The Netherlands: Mosmans, 1928.

Michell, J., and R.J.M Richard. *Phenomena: A Book of Wonders*. London: Thames & Hudson, 1977.

Nageleisen, J.A. *Charity for the Suffering Souls: An Explanation of the Catholic Doctrine of Purgatory*. Rockford, IL: TAN Books, 1982 (Orig. pub. 1895).

Cardinal Newman, J.H. *Sermons Bearing on Subjects of the Day*. 1857.

Owens, J.E., E.W. Cook, and I. Stevenson. "Features of "Near-Death Experience" in Relation to Whether or Not Patients Were Near Death." *The Lancet* 336 (1990): 1175–77.

Prévot, A. *Love, Peace, and Joy: Devotion to the Sacred Heart of Jesus according to St. Gertrude.* Rockford, IL: TAN Books, 1984 (Orig. pub. 1911).

Probst, Ch. "Nahtod-Erlebnisse (NDE's) aus der Sicht von Neurochirurgie und moderner Hirnforschung" (Near-death experiences from the viewpoint of neurosurgery and modern brain research). In *Dem Schönen und Heiligen dienen, dem Bösen wehren* (Serving the beautiful and sacred, resisting the evil), edited by N. Esser. Sinzig, 29–43. Germany: Sankt Meinrad Verlag, 1977.

Raupert, J.G. *Die Geister des Spiritismus: Erfahrungen und Beweise* (The spirits of spiritualism: Experiences and proofs). Innsbruck/Vienna/Munich: Tyrolia Verlag, 1930.

di Rocca, A. *Mutter Anna Maria Lindmayr O.C.D.: Eine barmherzige Helferin der armen Seelen* (Mother Anna Maria Lindmayr: A merciful helper of the poor souls). Gröbenzell, Germany: S. Hacker, 1974.

Rogalewski, Father T., M.I.C. *Lumen Marianorum: Stanislaus Papczynski.* Stockbridge, MA: Marian Press, 2001.

de Sales, St. Francis. *Treatise on the Love of God.* Rockford, IL: TAN Books, 1997 (Orig. pub. 1616).

Schmidt, W., S.V.D. *Der Ursprung der Gottesidee* (The origin of the concept of God). Münster, Germany: Aschaffendorffsche Verlagsbuchhandlung, 1926.

Schouppe, F.X., S.J. *Purgatory Explained.* Rockford, IL: Tan Books, 1989 (Orig. pub. 1893).

Schug, J.A., O.F.M. Cap. *A Padre Pio Profile.* Petersham, MA: St. Bede's Publications, 1987.

Schut. Results of a study reported in *De Telegraaf,* March 3, 1990. Vrije Universiteit/Free University, Amsterdam.

de Ségur, Msgr. L.G. *L'Enfer* (Hell). Paris: Tolra, 1876.

Siegmund, G. "Das Fortleben nach dem Tode im Lichte des Phänomens von eingebrannten Händen" (Survival after death in the light of the phenomenon of the burned-in hands). In *Fortleben nach dem Tode* (Survival after death), edited by A. Resch, 473–503. Imago Mundi, vol. 7. Innsbruck, Austria: Resch Verlag, 1981.

Siegmund, G. Daemonologie heute (Demonology today). In: E. von Petersdorff, *Daemonologie,* vol. I. Stein am Rhein (Switzerland): Christiana Verlag, 1982, p. 380-425.

———. "Das Phänomen der eingebrannten Hände." *Algemeine Zeitschrift für Parapsychologie* 3 (1981): 142–51.

Staudinger, O., O.S.B. *Wie dankbar die armen Seelen sind* (How grateful the poor souls are). Wels, Austria: Reisinger, 1977.

An Ursuline nun of Sligo, Ireland. *Stories of Purgatory and What They Reveal.* Rockford, IL: TAN Books, 2005 (Orig. pub. 1904).

Wagner, H. *Das grosse Wagnis* (The great venture). Vol. 1. Altötting, Deutschland: A. Ruhland, 1990.